C000175082

Becoming Myself

The True Story of Thomas Who Became Sara

Sara-Jane Cromwell

Gill & Macmillan

Gill & Macmillan Ltd
Hume Avenue, Park West, Dublin 12
with associated companies throughout the world
www.gillmacmillan.ie

© Sara-Jane Cromwell 2008
978 07171 4388 7

Type design: Make Communication
Print origination by Carole Lynch
Printed and bound by ColourBooks Ltd, Dublin

This book is typeset in Linotype Minion and Neue Helvetica.

The paper used in this book comes from the wood pulp of
managed forests. For every tree felled, at least one tree is
planted, thereby renewing natural resources.

All rights reserved. No part of this publication may be copied,
reproduced or transmitted in any form or by any means,
without permission of the publishers.

A CIP catalogue record for this book is available
from the British Library.

5 4 3 2 1

Contents

Acknowledgements

A joyful and pleasant thing it is to be thankful.
[PSALM 147:1]

I am eternally grateful to quite a few people who have not only made it possible for me to survive, but who have also helped me in my journey back to myself. Some of them don't even recognise the measure of their own contribution to this story and for some their modesty would not allow them to admit to it, but I insist on acknowledging them, precisely because they are so worthy of it for all they have done for me and what they mean to me now.

First and foremost, I am indebted to my friend, Kathy O'Donovan, who has had to cope with so much over the past eight years, especially the earlier and less pleasant stages of my transition. Kathy was also by my side on no less than four occasions when I tried to commit suicide. I deeply regret putting her through these experiences and as my friend, I can only love her and cherish her all the more for it. Kathy was one of the first people who taught me to think better of myself and of my abilities and who encouraged me to deal with my situation once and for all. She recognised very early on that I was a female and that I was deeply depressed because of it. There are simply no words adequate enough to thank her or to pay tribute to her for all that she has done for me.

Others I would like to acknowledge and thank are: Conny and Frank Ovesen at Flexa Furniture and Ivan and Karen

Nixon at MHC Shopfitters. They started out as my clients and then became good friends. They are also the first clients I told about my situation. They were so understanding and accepting of me and never once allowed it to affect our business relationship; if anything, that relationship was greatly enhanced by their generosity and I shall be forever grateful to them for it, especially as it gave me the much-needed confidence to go on in my business when it would have been so easy to panic and give it up. Thank you.

I wish to extend my warmest appreciation to my neighbours in Midleton who have been nothing but kind to me during the very difficult, and to be honest, frightening period of my transition. In particular, I would like to acknowledge the following: Gail, Lucy and Victoria Peters, who were the first of the neighbours I told and who have since become my friends; also, Geraldine, Jim and Mark who gave me a most enjoyable and joyous Christmas in 2004. To Michael, Kathleen and Katy Noonan who have been very supportive, as have Geraldine Mahon and her sons and Pierre, Marie and all their family. I also want to mention my neighbours, the Shortiss family, who have been exemplary in their kindness towards me. I have no doubt that some of these fine people will be more than a bit embarrassed to find themselves included here, but they thoroughly deserve it.

I am also indebted to Fabian and Sinead and Ruey and Geoff, who were my old neighbours in Castlemartyr. They have been nothing but supportive of me and fought over who was going to have me for Christmas dinner: I never realised I was such a sought-after guest! They made me feel very special and I had a wonderful Christmas with them back in 2005, which certainly helped me through what was one of the most stressful periods, and I am extremely grateful.

I am also grateful to the media for the sensitive manner in which they dealt with the issue of my gender dysphoria and for giving me the opportunity to tell my story in a totally dignified fashion. In particular, I would like to acknowledge the production team on the *Big Bite* show on RTÉ, Lara McCashan of the *Irish Independent*, David at Cork 103FM, and Alice de la Cour and Helen O'Callaghan of the *Irish Examiner*.

I would also like to extend my appreciation to my publishing mentor, Rachel Pierce, not only for believing in this project but because of the efforts she has made in helping it to see the light of day, and to Cormac Kinsella for having the foresight to pass it on to her.

I must reserve a special place for Liam and Sheena Joyce, for being the very best example of Christian love and friendship that I ever experienced since becoming a practising Christian, twenty-four years ago. It was Liam who first recognised very clearly that I had a strong feminine side. He knew there was something fundamentally different about me and that my plan to go to Bible college and into the ministry would be disastrous, not just for me, but for all those who would be under any ministry in which I served. He exercised great Christian compassion, foresight and courage in ensuring that I was not accepted into college, acting out of my best interests and for this I am profoundly grateful and deeply proud to call him my friend.

And to the countless others who have made a contribution to this story, a heartfelt thank you.

Introduction

The Beginning of the End

There must be a beginning to any great matter, but the continuing unto the end until it be thoroughly finished yields the true glory
[SIR FRANCIS DRAKE]

AUGUST 2003

It is a long drive from Cork to Dublin and it is normally a tiring trip, but such was my sense of anticipation and anxiety on that day, I hardly noticed. In fact, the entire trip was no more than a blur. All I could think about was what the doctor would say. I was due to see him at 2 p.m., but he was running late, which made me even more anxious. My chest was tight, I was short of breath and my heart was beating too fast.

I had very mixed feelings about what the doctor was likely to tell me. I wanted him to tell me I was a cross-dresser because that would make my life so much easier, but at the same time I knew I was going to hear the truth spoken for the first time in forty years. I shifted restlessly in the chair in his office, willing him to come into the room. I just wanted him to tell me what was wrong and how to fix it.

For over four decades I had lived a life that felt like a lie; I felt as if I'd been cheated out of life, now here I was, sitting in this chair and waiting for a verdict. This was the moment it all boiled down to: this one particular moment.

Dr Kelly sat back and smiled at me; I sat there as if some-one had pressed the pause button. 'Well, Sara, you probably already know what my diagnosis is going to be. It's gender identity disorder. I'll be writing to Dr Donal O'Shea, the endocrinologist at Loughlinstown Hospital to start you on your hormone treatment.'

Gender identity disorder; I hadn't heard the term until then, but those words would become the defining phrase of my life. Gender identity disorder isn't about cross-dressing or lifestyle choices or sexuality; it's a medical condition. In people like me — women born in men's bodies — the hypo-thalamus in the brain is formed differently *in utero* and is characterised female. So, while I was born with a male body, I had, to all intents and purposes, a female brain: wrong body, wrong life.

Throughout my life I have tried to feel like a male and live like a male, but I have never believed myself to be a male — even though I have been a son, a brother and a husband. My truth is that I am a female living in a male body, and this little fact has affected every minute of my life until now, and will no doubt do so for the rest of my life, too.

I never asked to be born like this, but I was and I am trying to make a new life for myself. They say a woman should never tell her age, but I am proud of the fact that I have survived against the odds to reach 46 — albeit living the wrong life in the wrong body, just because nature designed me differently.

This story is about what it was like to grow up in the wrong body and to suffer the effects of being different in other ways that many found so unacceptable, condemning me to a life of abuse, ridicule and rejection. But this is also a story of triumph and hope. A story that I hope will inspire others to believe that life really can get better and that it is worth living, despite all the difficulties. It is a story that shows the importance of being true to oneself, regardless of the price that has to be paid as a result.

For me, there is great solace in knowing I am not alone; we're not alone. There are countless thousands of people out there who were born different and are living with this, with varying levels of success. This story is dedicated to them. It's a long story, and although it doesn't start there, it ends in a place of hope and joy.

Over the past five years I've been trying to be myself and to find friends who can love the real me. It hasn't been the easiest of paths to walk, but it has taught me so much about life and love, about men and women, about hope and achievement. So, this story is the story of my transformation, from a victim of abuse to overcoming that abuse, from false self to true self. That transformation has physical aspects — hormone and bodily changes, hair, make-up, voice — but more important are the changes inside, the changes in my spiritual, inner self. Those are the changes that have given me new ways of thinking and happier ways of being. Those changes allow me to say now, today: *Who am I? I'm Sara-Jane and I'm very happy to be alive, very happy being me, and very happy to meet you.*

Welcome to my life!

Part One
Early Days

Chapter 1
I'm Here, But Who Am I?

I do not love him because he is good, but because he is my little child

[RABINDRANATH TAGORE]

'There is something I have to tell you about why I've been the way I have been towards you all this time. I always resented you, since you were a baby. I've never been able to explain it to myself, but I have resented you and there are times when I still do.'

My mother told me this when I was forty-two years of age. Finally, I felt vindicated by the knowledge that I had not been imagining it all these long years. Feeling that she really never loved me and that she really didn't want me around. The reason why is harder to explain, although I know that at the time of my birth, my mother's life was far from easy.

Even before I was born, events in my mother's life were conspiring against her ever wanting or accepting me as one of her own. Like so many other women, she, too, had her dreams and ambitions. And like so many other women at the time, she had her dreams and ambitions crushed and destroyed. I know that she had a dream of becoming an interior designer, for which she was ideally suited. And no doubt she had a dream of a fulfilling marriage and of raising a healthy, happy family, but this dream was also shattered. These crushed hopes undoubtedly led to great and lasting feelings of disappointment, resentment and bitterness. All of this was crystallised during a series of tragedies which occurred around the time when I was born and I am sure that they contributed to my mother's resentment of me.

My life started in the Coombe Hospital on 26 June 1960. At least my male life started on that date. When I came into the world, I was given the name Thomas. I was two weeks overdue; a late starter. This late start seems to have been a dominant theme in my life. Apparently, I only came into the world following a scare from a German shepherd dog. My mother opened the back door only to be greeted by a rather enthusiastic dog that jumped at her and scared the living daylights out of her, literally! She went into labour and I was the result.

I'm third in a family of twelve, until recently, seven boys and five girls. But since my diagnosis there are six boys and six girls. It was often said that we were a football team plus one. There were five boys before the first girl arrived. Apparently, being third in line is not the best place to be, especially if you're the third boy.

I was barely two months old when my mother fell pregnant again and this alone doesn't bear thinking about. She simply hadn't the resources to look after three of us, never mind four, but that never mattered in Catholic Ireland of the 1960s. All that mattered was that women accede to the sexual demands of their husbands. They were machines for producing Catholic babies and they did so efficiently and without question.

Women were expected to satisfy their husband's conjugal needs without any regard to their own or to the dire consequences of constantly producing children for which they could not adequately provide. And if these women failed to satisfy their husband's needs, well, then they were effectively raped. I did not visually witness such rapes as a child, but I certainly heard them, just feet away from where I slept, and was terrified. I heard my frightened mother plead with my father not to come near her as it was too soon after having yet another baby. Then I heard the smacks and the shouting at her to 'shut the fuck up!' Then there was crying, then whimpering, then silence and then the creaking of the bed and then total silence and I went to sleep crying for her. I cry for her now.

Before my parents moved into their new house in Ballyfermot, around the time when I was born, they had lived in married quarters in McKee or Collins Barracks, as my father was in the Army Motor Squadron and later joined the military police. And it was here that they were to experience some of the most traumatic events of their lives.

My father was staying in McKee Barracks the night before he was due to fly out on a tour of duty to the Congo with the United Nations. On that fateful day my mother learned that a man who had raped her some years earlier had moved into the neighbourhood. Not surprisingly, she had a breakdown, putting her hands through the glass window of our front door. My father was called home to take care of her and she was taken to St Loman's Hospital. As a consequence, my father's best friend was sent to the Congo in his place.

This friend would be killed, along with nine others, during a massacre at Niemba in September 1960, barely three months after I was born. It is almost impossible to imagine the impact this must have had on both their lives. They also knew some of the other soldiers killed, which only served to multiply their sense of loss and sorrow.

It is hard to think that they did not blame themselves in some way for their friend's death and that they were not wracked with guilt for a long time after the event. I know for certain that my mother attributes these events and others for causing my father to 'go off the rails'; what we now know as post-traumatic stress disorder. Of course, such a diagnosis did not exist then and those suffering from the condition received absolutely no help whatsoever. She assured us that our father was not always the violent man we knew him to be while growing up; that in fact he had been a very different man before these tragic events occurred.

I can say with a high degree of certainty that the difficult relationship that developed between me and my mother has its roots in this particular period of time. Although I find her animosity towards me, that bordered sometimes on hatred, difficult to understand. I remember a woman who made it abundantly clear that she did not want me and did not love me and is best summed up in her own words and through gritted teeth: 'I had twelve mistakes and you were my biggest mistake of them all!' In her bitterness and disappointments, she was all too human and imperfect, just like the rest of us.

My father remains something of an enigma to me and, like my mother, I feel that I hardly know him at all. I never had the kind of relationship with him that would allow me to get to know him better. What I do know about his earlier life comes from my mother and one of my brothers. He came from County Louth and had three other brothers that I know of. From what I've learned, he also had a terrible life: he was sexually abused while growing up and had more than his fair share of brutal beatings.

He spent long periods abroad on UN duty and when he was home, he was in the Curragh or on weekend camps with the army. When he wasn't away with the army, he was working on nixers for the owner of the local pharmacy. If he wasn't working outside the home, then he was working at home, painting, wallpapering and building the kitchenette, which I helped him to build. At one stage, he left the army for a number of years and went to work in a local weaving factory, where I went to work some years later. I used to bring him his lunch while he was at work and remember being overawed by the size of the machines and the noise they made. And the fluff! He eventually went back to the army and joined the military police. I always associated his uniform with aggression and violence and of being told what to do without the right to speak up. Unlike many men of his time, he was not much of a drinker and rarely, if ever, smoked, though later on he smoked a pipe. This gave him an air of calm which I rarely ever experienced.

There can be no doubting that he was hard working and, in fact, he was truly gifted with his hands, in much the same way as my mother was gifted in her ability in interior design. It is fair to say that in another time and under different circumstances they both would have been hugely successful in business. But it was not to be. As with my mother, my father was a product of his own time and experiences and he certainly brought them into his marriage and into his role as a father.

Every time I hear the Furey's song 'The Oul Man', I am reminded of what I never had with my father and what I never will have with him. There are so many songs that are full of resonances of my younger years and they fill me with emotion as I recall the various experiences to which those songs relate. No doubt that's true of us all. Something that distresses me now is the way in which I look like him. I want to have no reminders of him whenever I look in the mirror, nor have people tell me I look the image of my father.

For me, everything I have come to know about my father, every personal experience I had with him, taught me how not to be a man. In fact, people have asked me upon hearing this, if this was the reason I felt I was a girl? My answer is emphatically *no*, especially as my behaviours were far too instinctive and natural and predated any conscious decision on my part *not* to be like him, or my brothers for that matter. The one thing I will say about him was that, unlike my mother, he was equal in the severity of the beatings he gave us. In other words, he was impartial in his brutality.

One exception, and something that used to bother me and my brothers when we were young, was the time he spent with the girls and not with us. He would have them sit on his knee and play with them. It never occurred to us that there was something else entirely going on and that far from having any reason to be envious of them, we would have every reason to feel the greatest sympathy; though in my case it was more like empathy for what they were enduring unbeknownst to us.

I was fortunate enough to receive some old pictures from one of my sisters some time ago. I am in just two of them: in one, I am three or four years of age and the other, I'm making my First Holy Communion. They are haunting pictures and have helped to rekindle some memories that both cheer and sadden me. Looking at these pictures it is possible to remember the better and happier moments when, as a family, we were physically, if not emotionally, closer. They bring back the sounds and activities that made up so much of our time together. It is nice to look back at pictures of my siblings before the rot had set in and they help to remind me of feelings of love and affection towards them that surprise even me.

Looking at the rounded faces of my little sisters and brothers, it is difficult to think that their lives and mine would become so divisive and so full of pain. Who would think, looking at them, that they could ever loathe each other and not be able to sit in the same room together; and all of this because of what has been done to them by two people, our own parents? The very things we share in common are also the very things that divide us and prevent us from getting close to each other, in the truest sense of the word. I still regret that.

My earliest memories of family life go back to when I was about three or four, before I started school. I remember going to the zoo and crying because I wanted to sit at the front of the coach. I got my way and was very happy. Another memory is of being taken to the army barracks for parties. We would be allowed to climb into the armoured cars and other military vehicles. These were pleasant memories, as were our trips to the seaside.

In some of the other photos, I am struck by several of my mother out of doors. She liked to travel and preferred that to being at home. There can be no doubting that bringing up so many children with so few resources between my parents had to be oppressive and led to them trying to get out of the house as much as possible, preferably without us in tow. They used to go off together on my father's Honda motorbike. One of their favourite places was the Embankment in Tallaght, where they went to see Brendan Grace, Barleycorn, The Bards etc.

But it is also clear from the pictures that she liked to take her children out and about. We were taken to Dublin Zoo, to the beaches at Gormanstown, Rush and Portmarnock, where our father tried to teach us to swim. Sometimes a row would ensue between them because my father either didn't want to take us or because he complained of not having enough money for petrol, which was often his cover for not wanting to take us. This wasn't a problem by the time the younger ones came along as we older ones were bringing home significant income, which eliminated my mother's money worries; something she never acknowledged.

So there were good times when I was a child. But there were also the darker, more distressing times that even now make me wince with pain and sadness. One of my most disturbing memories is of being locked into the bedroom for long periods of time. This was a common occurrence.

It is hard to describe my feelings aged four when I had been left behind by my mother, but I do remember feeling unwanted and abandoned and that I was nothing but a nuisance, something I was to feel many, many times since. I wrote my first ever poem on this very subject.

Big! With chalky brown walls;
'Go in and be quiet.' The key turns
In the lock and I'm alone.
What did I do to be left alone?
Please open the door, I'm only four.

Was it once or more? I can't always recall,
But I remember the tears and the fears.
What wrong did I do to be left alone like this?
Please open the door, I'm only four!

Being on my own was like an eternity.
I felt they had abandoned me, that they
Didn't want me. No-one talks to me, not a sound.
Just me, here, alone.
Please, open the door, I'm only four.

And now I see the prophetic vision of it all.
My life has been like that empty room, with
No-one there and no-one here. No-one wanting
To talk or play. No, I was getting in the way.
Please open the door, I'm only four
And I can't bear the loneliness anymore.

That room was empty, devoid of human care.
There was no-one there to love me.
And still I'm alone, with no family and no place
To call my home. The key is still turned in the door
And I'm alone.
Please, please open the door, I just can't take the
Loneliness, pain and rejection any more!

I don't know the reason why my mum left me in the room
that day and other days. Probably it was to go shopping or
maybe she couldn't cope with the house and with raising
four boys, and maybe she just needed her space. Whatever it
was, it made me feel totally alone and unwanted; feelings that
were to dominate my life.

From the earliest age I can remember the stress that was to
fill every nook and cranny of our house; a house that never
felt like a home. A house I was glad to leave when I was
nineteen years of age. This wasn't helped by so many people

living in such a small space. We lived in a two-up and two-down. We did have an indoor bathroom and toilet, but although the houses were considered quite modern for their time and a big improvement on what had gone before, it was completely inadequate to accommodate fourteen people.

Of course, there was no privacy to be had for anyone, including my five sisters, who had to share the same bedroom with their brothers. That can't have been easy for them. We slept in a double bed and bunk beds. Up to five of us slept in the double bed; three at the top end and two at the bottom. There were another five sleeping in the bunks, with brothers and sisters having to sleep together. This was the situation until we got the new bed-settee in the parlour and the eldest brother was moved down. Later, another was moved down and this gave some more space to those of us left upstairs. After the eldest brother got married and left the house, the second eldest then moved down and later I, too, was moved down to share the settee. The parlour was great, because we could leave the light on for longer and read. We also had the record player and radio unit in the parlour, which meant that we could listen to our favourite radio station, Radio Luxembourg and the European Top 40.

We would sleep under blankets and army overcoats. There was a constant battle to hold onto the bit of blanket or bit of coat. It was a constant tug-of-war trying to stay warm, especially in the winter months. There was no central heating in those days and the only fire was the one in the kitchen. There was an open fireplace in our bedroom but it was never used. Imagine waking during the night and in the morning with your brother's smelly, long-nailed feet in your mouth and sticking up your nose or cutting into your skin. Added to this were the broken springs that kept pricking us. It was so uncomfortable and very difficult to get a good night's sleep. At Christmas and Easter, though, we were bound to have clean crisp sheets and blankets. My mother would threaten us not to tear them by telling us that we were not 'to so much as breathe' on them. Of course, we would try to make a joke out of this by holding our breath.

During the earlier years the stress in our house came mainly from the rows and fighting between my parents, or, should I say, my father beating my mother and her screaming and begging him not to hit her. This legacy of aggression was to be passed on to some of my brothers; while I was to become very passive and open to physical violence from males and females alike. Some of the worst rows came around Christmas, when my mother would go all-out to get us the best of presents and the best of clothes. Christmas was the one time of the year when we were sure to have new clothes, in fact, new everything. But it would be spoiled by my father's shouting at my mother and my mother screaming with fear and pleading with my father not to hit her, but to no avail. When we heard the screaming and shouting we would start crying and then my mother would have to come and comfort us and try to reassure us that there was nothing wrong. But we always knew, and I began to hate my father for what he was doing to her.

But it really didn't take a lot to make either of them angry and resort to violence towards their children either. It could be something like soiling our clothes while out playing, or losing money while going to the shops. Even something as innocuous as coming home late from school or crossing in front of the television as my father was doing the Pools on a Saturday evening. On a number of occasions, they beat and berated me for wetting the bed. The bedwetting was, I think, because I lived in a constant state of emotional distress, partly because of my family, partly because of school and also because I had all the emotions and instincts of a girl, but without the right to express them.

I remember trying to resist reading girls' comics and magazines, but I always felt like reading them. I was in a constant state of uncertainty about who I was and who I was meant to be. There was the need to belong, but hating what I had to do in order to fit in. It was also around this time that I felt the growing compulsion to dress as a girl, but there were no clothes to fit me save those of my mother. So, when she was out of the house and I was alone, I would go to her room and put on her clothes and try to look feminine. I would try to put on her make-up, but not very well.

What was most fantastic about this was the feelings of wholeness and of being right within myself. These were precious times and I would volunteer to stay at home from school, knowing that my mother would go out for a few hours and this would leave me free to get dressed. Of course, there was always the risk of getting caught, but it was still worth it. My sensitive personality was also becoming more pronounced as I grew, along with my empathic spirit. I had a growing sense of being split in two, but without ever knowing why. The tensions became a constant in my life and left me feeling extremely unsure of myself in how I was to behave. I found myself preferring the company of girls far more than boys, yet still trying to fit in and be accepted as *normal.* These developments were to have a profound impact on my ability to cope with the treatment I received from my family and my mother and father in particular. And it especially affected the way I responded to the beatings and the verbal abuse.

My father took issue with my being so sensitive and gentle as did my mother and siblings and he was not averse to calling me a cissy, because of my very girlish ways of dealing with things, and the way in which I would cry when hurt, or when I felt my brothers and sisters were hurt. Whenever I came home from school, he would call me 'a fucking whinger', or he would tell me to stop crying or he would give me 'something to cry about'. Like the others, he chose to view my girl-like behaviour as attention-seeking on my part.

My mother knew that my father was extremely bad-tempered and violent; that he would give us severe beatings for even the most minor misdemeanours. If we did something wrong — at least in her eyes — my mother would threaten us with our father's violence. I remember the time I'd lost money while going to the shops and having to come home and tell my mother. Or the time I had money stolen from me and I tried to convince my mother that it really was stolen, knowing full well she wasn't going to believe me. I would receive the inevitable threat: 'Wait till your father gets home; he's going to fuckin' kill you!'

It is so hard remembering these all-too-frequent experiences and the absolute terror they instilled within me without becoming upset. I can still remember the times I would urinate in my short trousers while walking home from school, knowing that I was going to get a beating. The nearer I got to home, the worse the urinating became. When I'd get home, I would be sent straight to bed without any food and I would have to stay there until my father got home. My stomach would churn. No amount of anticipation could really prepare you for the roar: 'Thomas, get the fuck down here now. And don't have me to tell you twice!'

No matter how much I anticipated it and tried to prepare

myself for it, I was still completely frozen with terror. I knew that the only thing worse than delaying the inevitable was what would happen if I didn't go down straight away. While he was sitting there as a petulant god, I would be standing there and peeing on the floor in sheer terror at what awaited me. Sometimes, the only clothes I wore were my vest and underpants.

'Come here, you bastard. I said come here! I'll teach you to lose money. You're nothing but a fucking troublemaker. You bastard. I'll fucking kill you the next time you lose money … the next time to tear your clothes … you come home late from school again!' He would get up from his chair, taking the belt from his trousers. He would come at me with his fists, his huge fists pounding against my little head. His huge fists pounding my little face and me peeing again on the floor. 'I'll give you something to piss about!'

Shouting abuse at me while he pounded me. Telling me how worthless I was while he lashed his belt across my bottom, across my back and across my face as he lost control and started to kick me around the floor. At other times he would use a two-by-one piece of wood and beat me wherever he could inflict the most pain. Then came the kicking. He would kick me around the floor with his army boots; all the while shouting and screaming at me while I tried to get away, which just made him worse, more vicious.

While he was beating me to a pulp, she would be screaming: 'Don't do it, Frank. He's not worth it, the bastard! Frank, the bastard isn't worth it. Frank, please, he's not fuckin' worth it.' These words and the vehemence with which they were spoken still haunt and hurt me; still strike at my heart.

However, I wasn't alone in being beaten. One of the worst and most savage beatings I ever witnessed was that of my brother, Peter. He was given a flask to take to school, but unfortunately for him, he dropped it. Of course, it broke and he had to come home and tell my mother. She in turn told my father, who was repairing the television at the time. 'How did you manage to break the fucking flask?' he roared.

'It slipped out of my hand, Dad.'

'Come here, you stupid little bastard,' he shouted back.

Peter had a tendency to laugh whenever he was nervous or distressed and the more distressed he became, the more he laughed. My parents always interpreted this as him not caring, but nothing could be further from the truth.

My father went into a complete rage and started beating Peter with his fists. The more he did this, the more distressed Peter became. The more distressed he became, the more he laughed. The more Peter laughed, the more viciously my father beat him. The more he laughed, the more my father screamed, 'Cry, you bastard. Cry, you bastard!' He punched him, broke a stick across his back then proceeded to kick him with a viciousness I had rarely seen, even against me.

The reason I think that I remember this beating above all is that Peter was always my star. I loved him like none of the others. We were just eleven months apart in age, I being the older of the two. I loved his company and his cheerfulness. I loved being out with him amongst our friends and felt so proud to be by his side. Because of my own sense of inferiority towards him and my other brothers and sisters, it was vital to me that he accept me and that he would allow me to get close. We did play together a lot in the younger years: our beds were used very frequently during our playtimes. Peter and I would play a game called the Funny Men on the bed. We would pretend that we were working up ladders painting walls. Suddenly, we would push each other off the imaginary ladder to fall into a bath of paint. At other times we used the double bed as a pick-up van and the bunk beds as a double-decker bus. We would drive our Dinkies around the bedroom floor, imagining the legs of the beds as corners of high-rise buildings. However, as Peter became more aware of how I was perceived by others, as a cissy, as different, he started to avoid me at every opportunity and even joined in the name-calling and put-downs. We had come a long way from the days of playing the Funny Men and football and going on our long adventures together with our friends. Peter would be lost to me out of his need to be loved and to be popular amongst our friends.

My relationship with my brother Fred was fraught with sibling rivalry. We fought at every turn and it took very little to provoke either one of us to fight the other. He was eighteen months older than me and was understandably closer to our oldest brother James than to me. It seemed that no matter what I did, he had to find a way of beating me. I hated it and tried my best to avoid it and him, not an easy thing to achieve in such a small house and where we had to share the same bed.

Fred suffered terribly with asthma and frequently missed school because of it. He had very nasty attacks and on a number of occasions we thought he was going to die. As much as I didn't like him at times, I certainly didn't want that. And, in spite of my feelings towards him, I wanted to protect him.

My brothers — and sisters — and I spent the best part of nineteen years in our bedroom. It was this bedroom that kept our secrets, that witnessed all our emotional highs and lows and wherein we held our little confabs about the injustices that were so much a part of our lives; well, at least some of us. This was the room in which we expressed our joys and sorrows. The place in which we found comfort, but which also served as our prison cell. It was the holding area for those who were to be victims of the most vicious beatings and the place we would go to in order to soothe our wounds, both physical and emotional. It was here that I kept my record player, cassette recorder, records, cassettes and my wonderful books; the few that I had. The record player was on my side of the bed so I was able to listen to my music through my headphones. We grew up on all kinds of music including Jim Reeves, Perry Como, Nat King Cole, Slim Whitman, Dean Martin and Connie Francis, Glen Campbell and Patsy Cline, to name just a few. As we got older we developed our own tastes. Music was to be one of my greatest comforters and also my greatest inspiration for coping with all my difficulties.

After some time Peter realised that I had been getting out of bed after everyone else was asleep and he came downstairs to see what I was doing, which was cleaning the kitchen and sitting room. He kept me company some of the time and so we started to play football between the table and chairs which we'd placed at either end of the sitting room to act as goal posts and used a tennis ball as our football. It was very enjoyable and made us tired enough to go back to bed after all the work was done. It was a bit like the story of the 'Elves and the Shoemaker', except of course that this little elf was doing the domestics rather than making shoes for the poor cobbler. Looking back to those times, it is so obvious how completely natural it was for me to act instinctively as a girl and to play homemaker, because that is, in effect, what I was doing.

*

One exception to the stress of our household was Christmas, which could be truly wonderful. My mum would pull out all the stops to make sure it was the best ever. Christmas was the one time of the year — along with Easter — that we never wanted for anything. We loved to put up the Christmas tree and decorations and to see all the other preparations being made, including the puddings. I had a strong liking for raw pudding mix and used to go to where they were hidden in the kitchen and stick my fingers in and scoop out nice big amounts and eat them till I made myself sick, not realising that we would have none left for Christmas if I kept eating it. We loved putting up our Christmas stockings on the bed-posts and looking forward to the surprise fillings when we awoke on Christmas morning. They would be filled with Lemon's sweets and we would get stuck into them, even before we came down for our toys. We would sneak down stairs about six or seven in the morning, trying not to wake our parents. The atmosphere of coming into the sitting room and seeing all the presents under the tree was just the best thing ever and so very exciting.

Our aunts and uncles came to our house every year to say Happy Christmas and to get their Christmas drink. That was also very exciting. There was such a wonderful and for the most part, peaceful, atmosphere for these few days, before we would revert to what was to be our version of normality. We loved most of the Christmas programmes on the telly, especially *Wanderly Wagon, Ludín and His Magic Flute, Chitty-Chitty Bang-Bang, Top of the Pops, Mike Yarwood,* the *Morecombe and Wise Show* and so on. On Christmas morn-ing we would all be marched off to mass at Our Lady of the Assumption. We were like the Von Trapp children, all wearing identical clothes and shoes. The girls always looked so pretty in their dresses and lovely ribbons. I always loved looking at girls in their curls and ribbons and wondered why I couldn't wear them.

I was quite a performer and storyteller as a youngster. During the mid-60s, I would stand on the road and tell tall stories to whoever would listen, of how I saved my father's life while he was in the Congo with the United Nations. He was being crushed to death by a huge python and I would come to his rescue by getting a knife and fighting the snake until he released my dad. I was paid a few pennies for telling this story. I also sang 'Walk Tall' by Val Doonican and, 'Walking the Streets in the Rain' by Butch Moore. In fact, I got the nickname, 'Butch Moore'. These songs became my party piece whenever we had some special occasion. I loved to sing at special occasions, but was often upstaged by Peter, who would get in my way and put me off singing, normally with some kind of derogatory remark that had everyone laughing except me.

There is no doubt that times were hard financially when we were growing up. I can distinctly recall a period during the 70s when my father was taking home about £16 a week, which had to feed at least ten of us at the time. He had to work extra hours in order to supplement his income and to try to provide us with a decent living. It wasn't always possible and this necessitated the older children giving up school in order to go out to work for a living.

Our situation was made worse by my mother's constant borrowing in order to make ends meet. It was a case of constantly robbing Peter to pay Paul. It had to be deeply frustrating for him to see her spending money the way she did and yet she needed to do what she thought was right, based on the way she was brought up. It was a no-win situation for either of them.

My mum kept a beautiful house. Everything was immaculate. She had a definite talent for interior design, as amply demonstrated over the years with the various designs she came up with for the house. The house décor was kept up to date. I recall the very vivid colours on the walls and floors, which were typical of the 60s and 70s. We had linoleum in every room which made them very cold during cold months of the year. We couldn't afford carpets back then. Keeping up with the trends meant getting knee-high in debt and this affected how were dressed and fed. We never starved, but some of the meals were decidedly short on substance. My mother's need to keep up with the trends created problems for my father as he was the one who had to do the painting and decorating, and later build the new kitchenette. The debts angered my father greatly; as did the constant changes and they had ceaseless rows because of it.

The fact is, we were poor throughout my earliest years and into my early teens, and this was reflected in our meals and clothing and the fact that we rarely, if ever, got new books for school. We got a lot of our meals from the Stew House on Glass Lane. It was also reflected in the fact that all of the older boys never got to finish school. They were all taken out of second-level, except me: I left when I was just eleven years old. The truth is that school was never really a priority for my mother. She preferred to have us do the housework and go out to work as soon as we were old enough.

Some of us were expected to do housework when we came in from school, sometimes before we could eat. And we would be sent to bed around 6 or 7 p.m. depending on our mother's mood. There was very little time for doing our homework after our chores and even when we did, we would be too tired. This meant getting into trouble with the teachers. Sometimes my mother would not give me a note for the teacher even though it wasn't my fault that the homework didn't get done. Sometimes I would be slapped or clattered and then get lines to write:

I must do my homework every day.
I must do my homework every day.
I must do my homework every day.

When we went to the Stew House we would have to stand in a queue and we would be taunted by people passing by on their way to and from school. We would put in our three or four pots and out would come the aromatic smell of fresh, hot food. We would get large pots of stew and potatoes for just two shillings a pot. We also got corned beef and chicken-and-ham roll. The food tasted fabulous and it certainly beat the usual bread and jam, bowls of soup or bread and margarine which we frequently got as our main meals. The nearest we ever got to butter and ham was when we would have visitors. Sometimes, we would try and hang around until they left, to see if they had left any sandwiches behind. That was a rare treat.

A lot of our clothes came from the Iveagh Market on Francis Street, in the Liberties. They came to us via the O'Keeffe's from Ballyfermot Drive. Up the road they would come with their oversized Dick-Whittington-style sack, except it was a loud orange sheet with all the clothes inside. Of course, there was the usual mortification at the sight of the sack being taken into our house, but we weren't too mor-tified if it meant getting a new pair of much-needed shoes, albeit second- or even third-hand. Sometimes, I was so desperate to get a pair that I would pretend they fit, even though they were crushing my feet. I couldn't take any more of sticking pieces of linoleum tile into my shoes because of the gaping holes in my soles, or because the soles had come away and were constantly taunting me with their incessant flapping up and down. It was especially noisy when walking up the school corridors. *Here's flapping-soles Dunne!* I would be taunted. But wearing tight shoes was to prepare me for fitting into another form of tight shoes many years later, I suppose!

We had very little money so my mother would borrow money from Mr Beagle. He would come to the house on Fridays with a box of groceries. Sometimes, there would be long slim bars of Cadbury's chocolate and we would wait to see if we would receive a piece. Sometimes we did and sometimes we didn't. At other times she would borrow money from Mrs Tallan, a neighbour, or from men who would call to the house every Friday. It was at a young age that we were taught to lie; at least when it suited her to have us go to the door and tell the callers that she wasn't at home. I could never understand why it was okay for us to lie when our parents told us to, but that we were never to lie on our own account. When I questioned this double standard, I would be beaten and told that I was a 'cheeky little bastard'.

We did our weekly shop in the Elephant supermarket on Le Fanu Road. There we would buy thirteen sliced pans, along with all the other bits and pieces. We would live on this food for a few days, but there would often not be enough to last the week. So we had to get by on bread and jam. And that included sandwiches for work, which often amounted to nothing more than bread and margarine. Not much for a young boy expected to work twelve hours a day. And if we expressed our frustration or the fact that we were still hungry, our mother would make us feel guilty by calling us a 'shower of ungrateful bastards'. This was often accompanied by smacks across the head and face.

As children we thought nothing of exchanging our clothes for toys, as toys were hard to come by after Christmas. Every few weeks the Travellers would come round in their Ford vans or the horse and wagon. They had all kinds of toys, including cowboy hats, balloons, guns and holsters, planes to throw, wind-up helicopters, whistles and sometimes foot-balls and beach balls. It was so exciting when they came but, of course, our mother refused to allow us to exchange our clothes for toys; no surprise there, especially as our clothes were all hand-me-down and -down and -down again, but, on the rare occasions that we were allowed to exchange clothes for toys, there was so much pleasure to be had. Even then, I was disappointed that I couldn't trade clothes for girls' toys and had to settle for boys', but it was better than nothing.

The Ballyfermot I remember was new and bright, with rows of six houses, small front gardens and slightly larger gardens at the back. Wrought-iron railings separated each house and in the early years, no-one really bothered with putting up walls or fences. They weren't considered necessary then. The walls were pebbledashed, and everything looked the same. That changed over the years and, it has to be said, not for the better.

Every second week, Farmer John would come round with his large drums on his wagon to see if we had any waste food for his pigs. He had a small farm beside the canal. It was very exciting when he would allow us to climb up onto the wagon and travel along with him. Sometimes, he would let me sit up front and at others he would allow us to stay on all the way up to the farm. The Johnston, Mooney and O'Brien van was another visitor to our streets. It would stop across from our home and when the bread man pulled up the shutter, the aroma of fresh bread and cakes filled the air. Again it was rare, but every now and again my mother would buy short-bread fingers, chocolate éclairs and cream slices or batch bread. Those were the days when bread actually tasted like bread, so fresh it was still warm when buttered.

As we were poor, my working life started at a very early age. I was made to do a lot of the household chores from as young as I can remember, about seven or eight years of age. When I was around nine I would go up to Young's Bar on Le Fanu Road and mind the cars for the customers. When they went to their cars I would walk over and say, 'Excuse me mis-ter, I was minding yer car for you.' I normally received a few pennies, or a sixpence; sometimes as much as a shilling.

At other times I would go out on Saturday and Sunday mornings to work with the milkman. He would pay me sixpence but sometimes as much as one or two shillings. I would nearly always spend the money before going home because I knew my mother would take it from me and I would never see it again. When I would ask her where my money was, she would tell me to stop annoying her, or she would clatter me across the face and tell me to, 'shut up or I'll break your fucking neck', and if it wasn't threats, then it was reminders of how ungrateful I was for all that she had done for me.

Chapter 2

School and My
First Jobs

'Tis education forms the common mind,
Just as the twig is bent, the tree's inclined
[ALEXANDER POPE]

School started for me when I was just five years old. I
went to the Dominican Convent boys' school on
Ballyfermot Road. It was such a strange place and very
imposing to a young child. There were scary statues and long
corridors with polished floors. The walls were painted a mixture of the usual institutional cream or yellow on top with
blue or green on the bottom. The classrooms seemed very big
and contained large press units where all the books and
chalks were kept and there were long blackboards and sloping desks with wooden bench seats attached.

The strangest thing of all for me were the nuns with their
long habits and serious, unfriendly looking faces. The other
thing that was strange to me was sitting with so many boys.
Where were the girls? I felt completely cut off from everyone
and everything familiar. I had a strong sense of not fitting in
with my classmates and they weren't slow in recognising this.
Nothing made sense to me. Because of the isolation, I found
it very difficult to learn and at no time in my school life did

I feel natural as a boy, despite all my best efforts to fit in.

My mother was told by one of my teachers that there was something wrong with me: I should not be writing with my left hand and I should be discouraged from doing so, and that I was extremely sensitive for a boy. In those days, being left-handed was a sign that you were backward in some way. In school I would be shouted at if I was caught using my left hand, or I would have my hand slapped until it was too sore to hold a pencil. At other times I was made to stand in the corner with my face to the wall and to listen to the teachers and classmates calling me a dunce.

When I went home and told my mother that the teachers had slapped me, she would tell me I must have done something to make them hit me, so she would hit me too and tell me I was, 'nothing but a fucking troublemaker'. I was still just a child and I found this kind of treatment overwhelming. I learned from the earliest age that I was to have no refuge from the very people who were supposed to be my guardians, my protectors, my nurturers.

As I was left-handed, mealtimes, too, were a complete nightmare. If I was caught using my left hand, my mother would shout at me to use my right hand. I tried, but it was just so awkward and I had no coordination or strength to use it, so, I would quickly put the fork or spoon back into my left hand, only to have my mother or my father come over and beat me over the head and shout at me, calling me a 'cheeky little bastard!' or, an 'awkward little fucker'. While at other times my mother would grit her teeth and call me, 'nothing but a fucking antichrist! I'll break your hand if you don't stop using it'. This was extremely hard to cope with and I started to withdraw further into myself. It got so bad and mealtimes were becoming so stressful I was unable to eat properly.

Instead of chewing my food I would swallow it, in order to get my meals over with as quickly as possible to avoid getting into trouble for using my left hand. But my mother would shout at me: 'Chew your food and don't swallow it.' Or it would be my brothers and sisters squealing and telling her: 'Mam, Thomas is using his left hand', or, 'Mam, Thomas is swallowing his food'.

My mother's difficulties with me grew worse after she was told by some teacher that I was 'mentally retarded' or 'remedial'. Back then there was no real distinction between the two. They both meant the same thing to an uneducated parent and siblings. I had to be taken to the doctors in Thomas Street and the St John of God hospital so they could check me out and get me to do different tests to assess my mental abilities.

I was able to do them okay and I was given a bag of sweets by the doctors. But at home and in school I was treated as anything but normal. It got out that I was supposed to be retarded and this led to years of bullying. I was frequently referred to as the 'retard', the 'spa' or the 'head case'; all serving to remind me that I was abnormal. To add to my woes at this time I was taken out of my class and placed in a special class. The teacher was a kind, elderly lady and she would give me sweets if I would go to her classroom, but, conscious of the fact that I would be bullied on my return, I did everything I could to resist and remain in my old class, but it was to no avail. I cannot remember her name, but I do remember her gentleness and kindly nature; a very rare experience during these years. She never shouted at me or called me names and that felt really strange at the time. I won a set of rosary beads while in her class; the first thing I'd ever won. I had to attend elocution classes where I learned to say: 'This, That, These and Those, That's the way the TH goes.'

Being told I was retarded then has had an horrendous effect upon my life ever since. It was used by so many people to put me down and to make me feel completely inadequate as a human being, that my life was useless and worthless and simply not worth the bother. It worked exceptionally well and served to hold me back for most of my life. So much so that, by the time I was sixteen, I was already contemplating committing suicide, or, at the very least, leaving home and changing my name. These feelings were to permeate my life, and stay with me for the next thirty years.

As a result of these feelings and the damage they caused, I spent most of my life trying to prove to myself and to everyone else that I am just as 'normal' as them. I thought that by working really hard, by spending my money on my family and so on that I would convince people that I was worth loving. But it never seemed to work, so I just worked harder and harder in a completely futile pursuit of approval. It was like climbing Mount Everest on my bare hands and knees. Every setback was perceived as yet another confirmation of how useless and unwanted I was.

At school we had to ask in Irish for permission to go to the toilet. We were often refused permission to go, which resulted in some of us wetting our pants. On one such occasion, when I was six, I asked for permission: *An bhfuil cead agam dul amach, más é do thoil é?* I was refused, but I told the teacher that I really needed to go and that, if I didn't, I was likely to go in my pants. She told me to sit down and stay quiet. I couldn't hold back any longer and excreted into my pants. This was humiliating, but it was made worse by the fact that it was diarrhoea and was running down the legs of my short pants. I stood up and told the teacher, who, without saying anything, left the classroom. While she was out my class-mates were laughing at me and calling me names.

The teacher returned to the classroom and called me out. 'Thomas, you are to go home with these girls.' She pointed to the two older girls she had brought back with her into the classroom. They looked like teenage girls. They had a pram and told me to sit into it, which I did. They pushed me along Ballyfermot Road and up the street where I lived, all the while laughing at what had happened to me. I reached home and was put into the kitchen sink, not the bath upstairs, by my mother. Nana and Aunt Nancy were in the kitchen with my mother and they all thought my predicament was some-thing to laugh about. I was told to strip and get onto the draining board. My mother proceeded to wash me in front of my nan and aunt. I was mortified and humiliated. Try to live that one down.

It was around 1967 or '68 when I first went to the De la Salle boys' school. Our special class was the last to move across and we were broken up into other classes. I arrived with some others in to Master Mullally's class. I was sent straight to the back of the class and left there. Any pupil who was thought to be slow was left behind. This led to me withdrawing more and more into myself on the one hand while desperately trying to fit in on the other, but I just didn't know how. I hated being in school, especially as this is where I experi-enced so much bullying. There was nowhere I could turn for refuge when trouble came.

Matters became so much worse when word spread that I was supposed to be retarded. People thought I was an easy target, and they were not wrong. When my classmates wanted to have a laugh, they would tell me I was 'nothing but a fucking spa!' Or, 'Dunne, you're a bleedin weirdo.'

Mr Mullally has stayed in my memory because he wore odd shoes and socks. The worst thing I could say about him was that he seemed almost completely indifferent to me and to the rest of the boys. This was better than those teachers and brothers who had no compunction about treating us harshly and humiliating us in front of our classmates. My left hand was frequently slapped by teachers and brothers until it was so painful that I could not hold a pen or pencil, never mind actually write with them. On other occasions, they would belt me across the back of the head or clatter me in the face, or pull me up by my ears and shout insults at me:

'You're completely stupid, Dunne, what are you?'

'I'm completely stupid, Master.'

'Say that louder, Dunne, we can't hear you.'

'I'm completely stupid, Master.'

'And why are you stupid, Dunne?'

'I don't know, Master.'

'Because you can't even use your right hand, isn't that it, Dunne?'

'Yes, Master.'

'Can't hear you, Dunne.'

'Yes, Master.'

'Now, get back to your seat.'

'Yes, Master.'

At this age, I was frequently kept back from school to clean the house. I also cooked for the whole family, dressed my younger brothers and sisters, changed their nappies, bathed them, took them out in their prams etc. And so, I would be slapped for missing school, because I'd been kept at home, and would be made to stand in front of the class until I came up with a believable excuse. The longer it took me to come up with something, the more I was slapped. Then there were the times when I would not be allowed to go to school until my work was finished. When I finally did turn up I would be slapped, clattered or given lines to do:

I must not be late for school.
I must not be late for school.
I must not be late for school.

Passing the girls' school was particularly difficult as it made me feel that I should have been on the other side of the wall and be attending the same classes as all the other girls. It was a deeply lonely experience.

There were many occasions during my schooldays where my mother's favouritism and, in particular, her dislike of me, were brought home to me, but I remember one incident above all others. I had been begging to go to see *The Vikings*, with Kirk Douglas and Tony Curtis. My brother Fred and I were promised faithfully by my mother that we could both go and see the film after school. I had to do a load of chores in order to be allowed go. On the day of the film I was hardly able to concentrate due to the excitement. I couldn't wait to go home for lunch and get the money to pay for my ticket and maybe a few sweets.

I came home and had lunch, or should I say gulped it down, such was my excitement. We went to my mother to get the money for the tickets, but she told us that only one of us could go to see the film and that someone was Fred. I wasn't taking it this time. I returned to school determined that I was going to see the film, so I decided to take matters into my own hands. I went to see the head brother, Brother Sebastian, and told him that my mother had told me to ask him if there were any spare tickets for the film, because she could not afford to send me to the pictures. It was, of course, a lie on my part, just as it had been on my mother's. She had the money, but just wanted me to be at home doing the house-work as usual.

Brother Sebastian gave me the ticket and I got to see the movie. It was spectacular and I enjoyed every minute of it, and it didn't matter that I had no money to spend on sweets; I got to see the film and that's all that mattered. I did this knowing full well there would be a major showdown when I arrived home, but, just this once, I was too determined to be afraid. It was amazing how much courage I found to stand up to my mother.

'Where were you until this hour?' my mother asked when I got back.

'I was at the film,' I said, trembling, knowing that I was in serious trouble and that I would be sent to bed without any-thing to eat and the prospect of a severe beating, along with the usual shouting and verbal abuse. I was determined that she was not going to win out this time, especially after what she had done to me in not keeping her promise. It was show-down time!

'And where did you get the money for the pictures?' She asked this with a tone that was clearly designed to terrify me into confessing. But I was adamant that I was not going to cave in. This was one beating she was not going to give me, nor for that matter was my father, not if I had anything to do with it.

'I won the ticket in a raffle,' I said.

'You're lying! Get down on your knees here and tell me the truth.'

I had to kneel on the hard floor in front of her and my smirking brothers. It was awful, but I was still determined. I'd never had a single victory or let-off with my parents up to this incident, but this time it was going to be different. I started to cry, but said nothing for a few moments.

'You will stay there until you tell the truth', she said.

So I thought for a few moments then said: 'I found the ticket in the school yard and brought it to Brother Sebastian. He told me to go round to all the classes and see if anyone lost it. Then he said if no-one claimed it, I could keep it, so no-one claimed it and I was allowed to keep it and go to the film.'

She remained unconvinced, but I remained steadfast and immovable. True to her word, she kept me kneeling there for what seemed like an age, but the longer I knelt there, the more courageous and determined I became.

Suddenly she said: 'I'm going to send your brother Fred in to see Brother Sebastian tomorrow and if he says you're lying, I'll fucking kill you, you little bastard!'

My brothers looked on with an air of superiority and were convinced that I was most likely going to get the hiding of my life the next day. But neither they nor I could have predicted what was to occur.

I was in class the following day, finding it impossible to concentrate on my lessons, not that unusual for me, but particularly hard when all I could think about was the inevitable beating that awaited me when I returned home; not to mention being sent straight to bed for the umpteenth time without dinner.

A pupil knocked on our classroom door: 'Master Mullally, Thomas Dunne is to go down to Brother Sebastian's office immediately.'

This is the moment I had dreaded. I was convinced that I was going to be exposed and pay the consequences. This filled me with the most awful terror and my stomach, not for the first, or the last time, was in terrible pain. I went down to Brother Sebastian's office and knocked at the door.

'Come in.'

I went in very sheepishly. 'Brother Sebastian, I'm Thomas Dunne and I was told to come down to you straight away.'

He looked at me with a smile and said: 'Thomas, your brother Fred has just been in to see me and told me this story about you finding a ticket in the yard and that you brought it to me and that I told you to go to each class to see if anyone had lost it. Now, Thomas, is that true?'

I was completely petrified; not only was this head brother going to cane me, but I was certain to get the hiding of my life when I went home. 'No, Brother Sebastian, it's not true.'

I then proceeded to tell him my sorry tale of how my mother had broken her promise to me and left me feeling upset at not being allowed go to the pictures and how I then came to see him and let on that my mother told me to ask him for the ticket.

He looked at me again with a smile and said: 'Well, now, Thomas, I told your brother that that is what happened, but you must promise me never to do that again. Do you promise?'

Of course I said, 'Yes, Brother Sebastian, I promise I won't do that again.'

He told me I was a good boy and gave me two lollipops, then sent me back to my class.

I felt euphoric and triumphant. I had just this once managed to withstand my mother's best and most determined efforts to get me to confess, waiting no doubt to give me another of her beatings around the head, coupled with the usual verbal abuse. But not this time, definitely not this time. This was to be one of those rare kindnesses shown to me during these tender years and I was grateful for it.

During the summer holidays, we would find so many ways to pass the time. We played soccer, street tennis, bulldogs, rounders, handball, etc. The smell of fresh Bitumen being poured between the splits in the concrete is something I loved, and still do. It made it so much easier to make calls in our tennis matches, as we could see the lines more clearly. We would go for long walks up to the canal and play in the grave-yard inside the Lawns at Le Fanu Road. Often, I went away on my own, walking, collecting bees in a jar and cycling around the Kylemore industrial estate.

But through all of this, I was secretly going through my own intense agonising over who I was truly meant to be. Any chance I got to play with the girls, I took it. We played a game called 'piggies' in which we would hop and push a shoe-polish tin between chalked squares until we got to the square at the top. It wasn't as easy as it sounds. What I loved about it was that it was mainly the girls who played it and so I could play with them without looking conspicuous. Yet, in spite of these happy moments, I hadn't the slightest idea why I should feel to completely at odds with myself, save what my parents, siblings, schoolteachers and schoolmates made me feel: that I was utterly stupid, retarded and worthless. I felt all that they made me feel, and yet these feelings of discon-nectedness were coming from a very different place. I think it was my emotional response to various life situations, along with a very non-male intuition which left me feeling that I didn't belong inside my male body. This feeling of being disconnected from my body was to get much stronger over the coming years and was to become a serious life-and-death issue; something I could not share with another living soul.

As a young boy with all of these conflicting feelings, I was nonetheless determined to fit in. Like many young boys at the time I joined the altar boys when I was eight years of age. I was completely devoted to being the best altar boy I could be and was awarded a prize for being the 'star altar boy' on a few occasions. This was one of the upsides to the job. Another upside was serving at ten o'clock Mass, because this meant getting off school for a couple of hours each morning. Sometimes, it would be longer because some funerals and weddings would be held after 10 o'clock Mass. But the 7.30 morning Mass was a scary experience, especially in the winter when I had to get up before 7 a.m. and walk down dark cold roads to the church. I was really scared of the dark and my imagination always ran away with itself, imagining people I knew who'd died coming out of their gardens and grabbing me.

As altar boys we would be treated to trips to the theatre and to see films in the Plaza cinema. It was while I was with the altar boys that I got to see *Ben Hur* and the *Ten Commandments* for the first time. It was amazing watching the chariot races in *Ben Hur* on the large curving cinema screen. It felt like the chariots were actually running over us.

Another benefit to being an altar boy was that my mother and brothers were less likely to give me a hard time once I was wearing my soutane and surplice. Wearing them made me feel very spiritual and close to God.

The Tridentine Mass was still being said during my first couple of years as an altar boy, in Latin and with the priest's back to the congregation. The people were like mindless drones as they repeated verbatim the same prayers Sunday after Sunday, but that all changed after the second Vatican Council, which had taken place a few years earlier in the early 60s. The altar was moved nearer to the congregation and the priest now faced the people. However, the ceremony was still very grandiose in nature and clearly intended to create a feeling of reverential awe on the part of the congregation. It worked, of course, and people enjoyed the spectacle, although they rarely, if ever, understood the full significance of what they were actually participating in. It was years later that I found myself questioning the value of all these rituals and their impact upon my life.

As an altar boy I had to attend numerous funerals; far too many for such a young boy. They had a deeply scarring effect upon my mind, bringing a terror of death into my life at a young age and adding to the darkness that was already engulfing my tender spirit. They made me far too serious and introverted.

As altar boys, we would have to attend the receiving of the remains on the evening before the funeral Mass. The bodies would be kept overnight in rooms at the back of the church, and if there were more than two coffins at a time, some would be left at the front side of the church. There were times when we would have to close the church, normally around 9 p.m., and when switching off the lights, we would have to check some of the rooms in the dark. It scared the living daylights out of me every time. Then there were those occasions when coffin lids were removed in order to allow loved ones to say goodbye for the last time. I found this a deeply emotionally disturbing experience, to stand there holding the crucifix and incense burner while staring at the corpses.

During these years, and for many years afterwards, I had

waking nightmares. They consisted of the most vivid images of me being buried alive, waking to the sounds of soil dropping onto the lid of the coffin. It terrified me so much that I would curl up against my brothers in the bed, but they would push me away, telling me I was a weirdo or they would ask me if I was 'queer or something?' I couldn't tell them why I was doing it because they would have just called me an attention-seeker. If I couldn't get comfort from being close to them, then I would curl up like a foetus and snuggle against my pillow, sucking my thumb, while the tears streamed down my face. I had to turn my screams and terror inward where no-one else could hear them. Eventually I would get to sleep, only to go through the same horror the next night, and again the following night.

The nights became weeks and the weeks became years. This continued right through until my early twenties, as did my thumb-sucking. (There is a photograph somewhere of me sucking my thumb while sleeping, taken while I was on two weeks' camp with the FCA in Longford.) The situation wasn't helped when we looked at horror movies late at night. I absolutely dreaded going to the toilet, because it meant going upstairs and expecting to see ghosts at the top of the stairs, or getting the fright of my life if the bulb had gone and I would have to look up and see the picture of the Sacred Heart on the wall, with the red light making it look very spooky.

I was sitting with one of my friends recently and sharing my experiences of the nightmares with her, when it suddenly dawned on me that it was not the fear of my own death that I was afraid of, but the death of my female gender identity; my female personality was slowly but surely being buried alive; literally! There is no other way of describing it other than that it was absolutely terrifying. Every day of my life terrified me and I hadn't a clue how to cope with it all.

It was while serving as an altar boy that I became convinced of my calling to the priesthood, but had to wait until I was seventeen before I could do anything about it. But I had a constant sense of spirituality from this time on. I had been so affected by my sense of calling that I engaged in religious role-playing in my bedroom with the help of some of my younger brothers and sisters. I would play the role of the priest saying Mass, using the dressing table as the altar and my brothers and sisters would act as altar boys. I guess they had a point when they thought I was weird. If I wasn't saying Mass then I would re-enact the crucifixion, using the bed as the Hill of Calvary. I even cried out: '*Eloi, Eloi, sabacthani.* My God, my God, why have you forsaken me?' These words were to prove prophetic.

Even at this young age I would enter the church on my own and stare at the crucifix. Everything else in the church seemed so meaningless and false. The only thing I could relate to was the figure on the cross. I felt we understood each other, that we had something in common. I would ask if my sufferings were a preparation for a life of service, and if so, what kind of service that would be. Being a Catholic and having spent so long as an altar boy it seemed logical that maybe I was being called to the priesthood. My sufferings made some sense in this context. Maybe I had to learn to suffer in order to help others who were suffering. Maybe I was learning to separate from my family, I thought, because I would have to work with so many people that I wouldn't be able to commit to a family of my own in the future. Of course, I now know that I was preparing for a life of a different kind, but it would be many years before I was to be able to live it, and so, for a long time, religion became my salvation.

It was around this time that I started to sense my feminine side in a more pronounced way than earlier in my childhood. It was becoming less vague, especially as I was beginning to feel increasingly physically abnormal. I couldn't understand why I had a penis instead of a vagina, and then I noticed girls my own age developing breasts and wondered why I wasn't. I became increasingly distressed but never dared to express my feelings to a living soul, especially as they already considered me to be odd. There was no undue female influence upon my life that could explain this and I tried to be a normal boy just like my brothers and friends. In fact just about everything I did throughout my entire life was aimed at proving to others that I was just as normal as they were.

I was about nine years of age when I started to wear my mother's clothes. I would be left alone in the house to take care of my younger brothers and sisters and to do the house-work, sometimes for hours at a time. I would go to my mother's bedroom and go through her wardrobe and drawers to find clothes to wear. She had lovely floral patterned dresses of crimplene, crêpe and chiffon. When I was dressed I would then experiment with her make-up. It is so difficult to explain the sheer joy and *knowing* contentment I would feel at these times. The experience was full of delight and terror at the same time. I was exhilarated and wonder-fully content being a girl for that short time, but I was also terrified at being found out. I was caught once by one of my brothers, but he never let on that he saw me. It was to be years before I discovered why he never said anything, and his reasons were to reinforce for me the fact that I wasn't dressing for kicks, but for an altogether more profound reason. The simple truth is, I felt like a freak inside while I was living, or should I say *trying* to live as a boy, but when I was dressed in my mother's clothes, I felt truly normal.

There were a few occasions when I was nearly discovered by my mother. I remember running and hiding in the wardrobe with my heart racing, waiting for her to come up the stairs and to open the wardrobe only to find me standing there in her clothes. However, not even this fear was enough to deter me from taking every opportunity to dress and be a girl; to be my true self, a girl with no name. That is what I was until my friend Kathy gave me my new name in 2003. These rare opportunities were to end after I started working and once I became a teenager, it was to be at least another ten years before the opportunity to be a girl, well, to at least *feel* like a girl, was to present itself.

One such occasion was during the annual Community Week in Ballyfermot. It was held during the summer holidays and there was a variety of activities, including soccer tournaments, fancy dress competitions and a fair. Community Week was a really big deal, a real coming-together of the community. We all joined in in cleaning our streets and putting up bunting. It was a time for taking pride in ourselves and in each other. Soccer tournaments took place in the Lawns. As much as I looked forward to it I was rarely picked for any of the teams, which made me feel left out, but I came into my own at the fancy dress parade.

One particular year, 1970–71, I dressed as Miss World. It was suggested to me by my mother for some particular reason. But I jumped at the opportunity because it was in keeping with my instincts, my growing sense of my own femininity. I was dressed in a striped swimsuit, tights, heels and a wig. The only thing that struck me after the initial nervousness was how natural I felt, for the first time in my ten years. It felt like

I was in a state of bliss. Unfortunately, it didn't last very long and was to become nothing more than a fond memory of one day in my childhood when I really knew who I was supposed to be. It was simply a wonderful experience.

There were times when I felt myself able to fit in with the other boys. During the summer holidays one of our favourite pastimes was to go up to the canal and play around the Seventh Lock. We liked to dare each other to walk across the narrow foot boards. This was a special thrill for me because I couldn't swim. I really did envy the boys who could be so fearless and jump into the lock and swim. I feel that the reason I still can't swim is because of the time that Joey Maguire pushed me from behind into the canal. I was about eight at the time. We were standing under the bridge and Joey was daring me to get into the water, but I was saying I didn't want to.

'That's because you can't swim,' he said.

'Yes I can,' I retorted, although it was a lie. I didn't want to be caught being a cissy.

'I bet you can't.'

'Oh, yes I can,' I said, adamant.

The next thing I knew, I was heading towards the water in a state of total panic. 'Jaysus! I can't swim, I can't swim! Get me out! For fuck's sake get me out, I can't swim!'

'I knew you couldn't bleedin' swim, you fuckin eejit!'

They pulled me out of the water but not before they had a really good laugh. I never learned to swim after that. I was like a ship that was off balance and kept keeling over to the right every time I tried.

We would go to the Gala cinema on a Saturday or Sunday for the afternoon matinee. We also went to the pictures shown in the playground hall. We saw all kinds of films, Westerns, war films and fencing films — as we called them. We would play out what we had seen in the films on the way home through the Lawns. We also watched *Lassie*, *Flipper* and the *Three Stooges*, to name but a few. We all wanted to be the Americans when playing out the war films and the cowboys in the westerns. Sometimes we went searching for vampires in the old graveyard. The graveyard was turned into a mound some years ago.

Another formative time for me was our holidays in Oakwood in Co. Wicklow and Coolure House in Co. Meath, organised by a local community group. We loved these holidays; I just loved being away from my parents and from all the stress and tension, the rows, violence and favouritism. I still remember our bedrooms in the cabins and the toilets and showers across the yard; the communal hall for our meals and the sitting room where we relaxed and had our dances. I loved Oakwood and still do. It was there I learned to love the songs, 'Matrimony' and 'Nothing Rhymed' by Gilbert O'Sullivan and 'Sylvia's Mother' by Dr Hook. I won a talent competition in Oakwood for singing 'Two Little Boys', by Rolf Harris. I loved the farm animals, the ducks and geese, the pigs and the donkeys, the sloping hills down towards the rushing river; walking across the river on the slippery stones. I envied the boys and girls who could swim in the deepest part of the river, and I especially enjoyed sitting by the riverbank watching them all jumping in and having such fun. It was all so lovely and relaxing and I really did feel free from the awfulness of my home life.

The last of my holidays was in 1972, the same year I left school and started my first job. The holiday was to be truly momentous. We were due to go to Coolure House in August and, needless to say, we were full of excitement and impatience. A few days before, I was trying to flush the toilet when the chain came away in my hand. I tried to put it back into its bracket, but while I was standing on the toilet seat, it split in two. My mother came home and discovered the broken seat. I was too scared to tell her what had happened and, as usual, she threatened us with another beating from our father. We were all under suspicion, but despite this I was just too terrified to own up. When we were summoned by him we remained silent. He then told us that we would not be allowed to go on our holidays. Still no-one came forward. He was relentless and we were all sent to bed without anything to eat. The next day we started all over again, after he arrived home from work. Needless to say we were disconsolate at the prospect of missing our holiday. Eventually, my brother Stephen went in and told him that he had done it.

'I fuckin' knew it was you, you little fucker!' my mother shouted.

When I heard this I started to cry for Stephen and rushed in to tell them that I was the one who broke the seat and how it came about, but as usual they would not listen to me. Stephen got the most savage of beatings. He was beaten with fists, then an army belt and then my father kicked him around the floor. I was having flashbacks to the vicious assault on my brother Peter years earlier. My father was determined to continue with the punishment against us so he forbade us to go on our holiday. It was a completely petty and unjust act. We pleaded with our mother to ask him to let us go. He eventually relented and allowed us to go.

We travelled to Coolure in a Ford Transit minibus. I remember us driving up what seemed like a boreen into a

wide opening at the front of the house. It was a mansion compared to what I was used to, with large rooms immediately to
the right and left as we entered. We slept in a communal bedroom. No sooner had I arrived, than I felt a strong sense of
elation mixed with an immediate dread of going home in a
few days. Anything was better than Ballyfermot and this was
paradise.

I went out to explore the grounds. At the rear of the house
was Lough Derravaragh; to the right were the stables, where
I met Angela. She looked after the horses and was very down
to earth. I felt really comfortable in her company. We had
discos in the big room to the left of the entrance and I
enjoyed the dancing. It was wonderfully peaceful and stress
free. I just loved it and hated having to go home.

One day, we were riding along the boreen and, coming
through one of the gates, one of the boys hit my horse's hind
leg. The horse bolted and the next thing I knew it was
galloping along the boreen. Someone shouted 'watch out!' I
stuck my head up and back to see who had shouted the
warning, then I turned back, just in time to see the branch
sticking out from the tree. The next thing I remember was
waking up in the arms of Angela in Our Lady's Hospital in
Drogheda. I had been unconscious for quite some time.

I awoke to the sound of Neil Diamond's *Hot August Night*
LP. I still remember listening to 'Crunchy Granola Suite', 'I
am, I Said', 'Canta Libre', but most especially 'Morningside', a
song about a man who made a table out of oak wood, but no-
one noticed the gift he had. He died alone and that made
such an impact upon me. I recognised myself in the man
who gave the best of what he had only to remain unwanted
and alone. And then there was 'Girl, You'll be a Woman
Soon'; except that I never did get to be a woman any time

soon. No prizes for guessing that Neil Diamond was, and remains, my favourite singer song writer, with John Denver a very close second. They sang to my soul.

I was the one who introduced the Bee Gees, Neil Diamond, John Denver and many others into our home. My brothers would let on that they didn't like them but when I wasn't at home, they would listen to my records. Sometimes, they would think I wasn't going to be there so they would play my records, only for me to arrive home and catch them. In fact we learned to gauge the state of each other's love lives by the music we were listening to at any given time. Peter was dating a girl from across the road and we could always tell when it was going well and when things were going badly. He would play my records until they couldn't be played any more.

Peter had this habit of rolling his head from side to side with the head phones on and singing at the top of his voice, while crying. We got a great kick out of this, especially when he would deny that he was even doing it. Despite the fact that he did ruin my records, I hated to see him go through the pain of his break-up. He had been with the same girl for a number of years and he clearly loved her very much. I always had a soft spot for Peter and tried to get close to him, but it wasn't to be. Like all my siblings, the need for my mother's approval meant that I was belittled at every opportunity. This was to be one of the greatest hurts of my life.

My entire childhood was notable for a complete lack of moral guidance from either of my parents. They issued their orders, but never felt it necessary to explain the reasons why we should obey their rules. It was supposed to be enough for them to tell us what to do and we would simply obey without question. It was a case of 'do as I say, not as I do'. It never occurred to them that we realised that they were applying double standards. We were not permitted to ask even the most innocent of questions or to make any kind of comment or complaint. Most of us lived in fear while a small number of us lived in sheer terror. Virtually every one of my brothers and sisters learned to keep their mouths shut — it was far more important to fit in and avoid vicious beatings than it was to have their own thoughts and opinions, to have their own minds — all except me. I just never believed that it was right for me to remain silent and I'm so glad I never did, despite the vicious beatings and other abuse I was to receive throughout my childhood and well into my adult life. I'm really glad I withstood all the attempts to get me to be something I'm not.

This phase of my life was to be marked by a growing sense of being disconnected from everyone around me but, more importantly, feeling disconnected from *myself*. Of course, I didn't know that it was really the girl inside me trying to live, but it was at this time that I started to wear my mother's clothes and to experiment with her make-up. It was also a time in which I began to develop a sense of my femaleness, but without really understanding what was happening to me. I began to develop the ability to relate to people on an unusually deep level and was able to see to the very heart of issues rather than engage in petty squabbling. I also developed an ability to strongly empathise with other people's suffering, especially other children, all of which might be considered 'female' qualities. But I received many put-downs, precisely because of the fact that I was so very different from everyone around me. So, the more they told me I was abnormal, the harder I tried to be normal. But the more I tried to be a boy, the more I felt like a girl; the more sensitive I was, the more they ridiculed and abused me. Growing into adolescence was to be a very traumatic and lonely time in my life.

The only real glimpse of light for me during these times was when I was kept out of school by my mother to do all the household chores while she went to visit her mother, or went into the city. It meant that I was home alone and could listen to my father's music. It also meant that I could dress in nice clothes and put on some make-up and feel like my true self, though it also meant being really scared in case someone would arrive home unexpectedly. But it was so worth it to have those all-too-brief hours alone and to express on the outside how I felt on the inside. They were the only times when I felt any real sense of being normal and fulfilled as a young girl. It was just so precious and so wonderful. No-one could hurt me during these few short hours of respite.

Of course, I hadn't the slightest idea why exactly it was that I felt this need to be someone else. What I do remember is that this entire period of my life was dominated by the most awful verbal and physical abuse, and I was to leave this phase of my life carrying a sense of worthlessness and rejection: I left my childhood without being able properly to read and write, or to speak coherently. And yet, my mind was able to articulate things to me in the most amazing inner voice. I could see things and understand truths that I was never supposed to see for one so 'retarded'.

As I entered puberty, I was also entering into an emotional wilderness, without any of the skills which would enable me to survive. I was entering into a phase of my life that was to see my female identity and nature become even more noticeable, but without ever being appreciated for what it really was. I didn't have the slightest hint that my mother and brothers and sisters had, in fact, noticed that I had very strong female traits during my earlier years. They would later comment on it when I received my diagnosis, but at this stage, they ignored them or used them as a justification for putting me down, calling me a 'cry baby' or a 'cissy'.

I spent the last six months of primary school working at home, cooking, cleaning, minding my younger brothers and sisters, changing their nappies, taking them for walks and entertaining them in whatever ways I could. Such was my desperation for my mother's acceptance that I was prepared to go to any lengths to win her affection. So much so that I would wait until everyone was asleep in their beds before getting up and going down stairs to clean up and get the kitchen and sitting room gleaming. I would wash all the ware, clean the cooker, do the dusting, wash and polish the floors and set the table for the whole family. I would then go to bed, hoping everything would be a pleasant surprise for my mother and that she would treat me better. It was a complete waste of time: but it took years to accept this. All my family commented about was my setting the table for left-handers! It drove them all crazy.

Chapter 3
Too Soon an Adult

Which of us…is to do the hard and dirty work
for the rest — and for what pay?
Who is to do the pleasant and clean work, and
for what pay?
[JOHN RUSKIN]

1972 was a momentous year. On Sunday 30 January, 13 people were shot dead by the British Army and the incident was to go down in history as *Bloody Sunday*. There was the burning of the British embassy and the throwing of thirteen coffins against the burning building. It was also the year in which eleven Israelis were massacred at the Munich Olympics and Michael Jackson made it to number one with his song 'Ben'. It was also the year during which I started work, at twelve years of age. As soon as we were able or showed a willingness to give up school, our mother made sure we started work and earned a wage to support our large household. Education was not a priority for my parents, and not one of my brothers and sisters was to finish school.

I was well below the legal age and my first jobs were very hard and the wages very low. In fact, I have often described my first years of work as something out of a Charles Dickens novel. There were no rights for younger workers back then. No matter how sick I was, I was still expected to arrive at work and put in a full day's hard graft. But, more importantly, in order to survive in the workplace, it was necessary to become an adult of sorts; all the talk was adult talk, all the humour, adult humour; all of which I was expected to keep up with, but which went completely over my head. I was lost and out of my depth. To make matters worse, I was becoming more aware of the fact that I was not developing physically as I thought I should. In other words: I wasn't developing into the girl I felt myself to be inside.

My first job was in a clothing factory on the Kylemore industrial estate. I started on a Monday and my wages were just £6.50 per week. My job was to press the hems of trench coats; an extremely repetitive and boring job. I had had a heavy infection by the Wednesday and spent a lot of time going to the toilet to blow my nose. It was very embarrassing and my boss noticed that I was leaving my post quite a bit. On enquiry into what was wrong I told him I'd had my appendix removed and that I was still in pain. Well, it was true and at least it sounded better than I just had a heavy cold. It worked, and I lost my job after just three days. He told me I should not be working until my scar had fully healed. Of course he was right, but my mother didn't see it in quite the same way. All I got out of the £6.50 was about 50p.

My next job was at Ryan's Petrol Station on the Rathmines Road. My wages there were £7.50 per week. I worked two shifts there, 7 a.m. to 3 p.m. and 3 p.m. to 11 p.m.; and I was still only twelve years of age. I had lied about my age. Because I was tall for one so young, I was able to pass myself off as a teenager of 14 or 15. It meant, of course, getting up very early in the mornings to get the number 18 bus from Kylemore Road, then walking from Rathmines Garda station to the end of the Rathmines Road, another mile or so away. I was given just 50–75p from my wages by my mother, and from that I had to pay my bus fares and for some of my lunches. Also, I would have to make my own lunches and do my own chores either before going into work for the three o'clock shift or when I came home from doing the early shift. It didn't matter how exhausted I was, I still had to do them and often before getting anything to eat. I felt that this was terribly unjust given that my other brothers did not get the same treatment. And some of my brothers who could do the chores were allowed to get away without doing them. But things were changing.

The more time I spent out of the house, the more remote I felt from the family and experienced a sense of genuine elation at not being under my mother's control. And there was no-one to squeal if I did something wrong or for making mistakes. For those few hours at least no-one could give me a hard time because I was using my left hand. I could have conversations with adults without worrying about what they would say to my mother. And I would jump at the chance of doing overtime as it meant another 50p or so for my pocket money and it meant being out of the house even longer.

I met Marie who worked across the road in Martin's rental shop. She was about 17 and I really liked her. I would look for any opportunity to go over and have a chat. I always liked talking to other girls, though it always seemed strange to be doing this as a *boy*, or at least in a boy's body. But I had no sisters at this time that I could talk to, as they were all younger than me, which deepened my ever-increasing sense of loneliness and isolation. As awful as the isolation felt, though, it was still better than being in such a stress-filled house.

I needed to earn more money because of having so little pocket money — the little I had was being spent on my younger brothers and sisters and on buying my mother gifts for this that and the other — so I came up with the idea of washing cars in the garage. It was not being used for anything else and so I decided to make use of it. I started by asking the man who owned the rental shop across the road if he would like to have his car washed. He said he would and I was delighted. I told him it would be 50p and he agreed.

'Make sure you so a good job now.'

'No problem...'

'And make sure you wax it when you've finished washing it.'

'Okay.'

'Put plenty of elbow grease into it.'

'Okay, but where will I get the elbow grease?'

'The lads in the auto shop two doors down will get it for you.'

So I confidently strolled into the auto shop. 'Heya Paddy, Martin from across the road wants me to use elbow grease for waxing his car. Do you have any?'

Paddy looked at me in disbelief, but never let on. 'I don't have any here at the moment. If you come back later, I'll make some up for you.'

'Okay, see you later. Oh, by the way, how much is it?'

'Don't worry about that.'

'Okay, thanks, see you later.'

And I did call back later, looking for the elbow grease. And when I found out that he had no elbow grease I was left puzzled at what to do next, so I went to tell Martin. He just smiled and said not to worry. It never occurred to me that they were having a bit of fun at my expense.

As the oil crisis of 1972 deepened and filling stations ran out of petrol, causing some to close down, I was let go from my job, but I got another one just as quickly, in Robinson's Butchers on Dunville Avenue in Ranelagh. I worked on the delivery van and travelled to various locations, one of which was an orphanage in Co Wicklow.

I enjoyed working in the butchers, but I could have done without having to get the heads of the cows out of the freezer first thing on a Monday morning. Another of my jobs was pickling the corned beef and bacon, while another was making the sausages.

Mary came in and did the canteen work and made sandwiches for our breaks. She would fry the freshest bacon and sausages and put them between slices of white bread and butter. They were fantastic. We could smell the lovely sausages and bacon and hear the sizzling as they fried. I looked forward to going to work, knowing what awaited me at my ten-o'-clock tea break, especially as I rarely had a decent breakfast at home.

Working in Robinson's nearly cost me my life. I had just started work on a Monday morning and was told to go into the freezer to take down a carcass and bring it into the shop. When I went to lift the carcass off the hook, I received the most awful electric shock. The lads knew the bars holding the meat were live and thought it would be a great laugh to see me get such a shock. Needless to say, I wasn't very impressed.

Later that same day I was cleaning the yard and decided to wash it down with water from the tap against the yard wall. I had forgotten about the earlier incident and never made any connection between the live bars in the freezer and the water coming from the tap. In fact, the first time I turned the tap, there was no problem. However the second time I put my hand on the tap, the electric current went right through me. I could not get my hand off the tap and felt my life draining away as I was being electrocuted. I was only saved because one of the workers, Richard, who came out of the shop just in time, saw what was happening and grabbed a wooden bench, using it to wedge me away from the tap. I was in the most indescribable pain, yet no-one made sure I was taken to the hospital; not even my mother when I told her what had happened. I have suffered with palpitations and a twitch ever since. I was made to go to work the next day despite still being in a lot of pain.

The palpitations got worse by the day and came to a head on Christmas Eve, 1973. I was helping my mother clean the house and prepare for Christmas morning. It was about 9.30 in the evening, when it felt for all the world like my heart had finally stopped and I was dying. I completely freaked out and kept screaming, 'I don't want to die, I don't want to die.' It was truly awful. My parents decided to leave me until the next morning and, if the problem persisted, to take me to Our Lady's Hospital in Crumlin. Christmas morning came and I was no better, as I had spent the night afraid to go to sleep for fear I would never wake up again. My father saw that I was in a very bad way and so took me to the hospital early that morning. They diagnosed me as having palpitations and advised my parents to keep stress to a minimum: fat chance of that happening.

I lived in a constant state of fear from that time on. It was to be many years before I could stop checking to see if I still had a pulse. Added to this I was suffering from waking night-mares, which were worsening and becoming more frequent, keeping me in a morbid state of fear. I am not sure if my palpitations were simply as a result of that electric shock, or the growing tension I felt between my 'real', female, self and the young man I was supposed to be to everyone around me. I was beginning to feel more like a freak because my body wasn't doing what I was expecting it to do, and these feelings grew by the day.

After some months working at various jobs, having been laid off by Robinson's, I found myself unemployed, so I called into Weavex on the Kylemore Road and asked if I could speak to the manager. I was led up to Bernard Nolan's office. He was sitting with his back to me and didn't turn around when I spoke: 'Excuse me, mister, do you have any jobs?'

'What age are you?'

'I'm fifteen,' I lied. In fact I was still only fourteen.

'What's your name?'

'Thomas Dunne.'

'And where do you live?' I told him my address and he just said, 'Start on Monday at eight o'clock.'

'Thank you,' I said and left the office, before he had a chance to change his mind. I never let on that my father had worked there previously, because, even at fourteen, I wanted to get on in life on my own merit and not have to use other people's names.

On my first day in Weavex, I was a cause of curiosity as some of the other staff recognised me as one of the Dunnes and remembered that my father had worked there some time earlier, so I was bombarded with questions. I was told to lift some large boxes and my word were they heavy; so heavy I don't know where I got the strength to do it, but I had to, it was as simple as that.

One of my jobs was to be the 'nipper', which meant doing the shopping for the staff. I had to make a shopping list and take it to the shops on Decies Road. I would leave a large order into Borza's, the chipper, then to the Londis supermarket. I would make my shopping list out on pieces of cardboard, starting in the packaging and despatch department where I worked, then out to the department where they made the warps and quills and where the looms were for making labels; then into the weaving department, or 'shed', as it was then called. It was an amazing experience to walk amongst all those looms with their loud repetitive clacking noise, so loud that you could hardly hear yourself speak and so you would have to shout at the top of your voice. It was strange being in the very place in which I used to bring my father his lunch and to meet the same workmates who worked with him and to be asked if I was his son. I was to spend the next five years of my life here: almost my entire adolescent life and entry into adulthood.

On one occasion when I was doing the shopping I was asked to get Durex! Of course, I hadn't a clue what they were and so asked the guy who wanted them. He told me they were like a chocolate éclair! I put them on the shopping list and handed it into the girl in the newsagent's, then left for the chipper. When I returned to the newsagent's, the girl asked me out loud what I wanted Durex for? I was very surprised by the question and tried to explain that they were some kind of chocolate éclair cake. She said, 'We don't sell them here, love. You'll have to go to the chemist for them.'

So I did, and much to my surprise, received the dirtiest of looks from the staff. 'We don't sell them here,' they said in scornful tones. When I returned to the factory, I told the guy who'd requested them, but all he did was laugh with his mates: 'Jaysus, Dunne, you're such a gobshite.'

On another occasion, shortly after I'd started in Weavex, I

was told by one of the fitters to go into the steam house and ask Charlie for a bucket of steam. On this occasion I was certain they were having me on and confidently said, 'Yis are having me on. There's no such thing as bucket of steam.'

But the fitter replied, 'There is, if you put a cloth over the bucket.' So, off I went again like the proverbial turkey to the slaughter and asked Charlie for the bucket of steam and if he would mind letting me have a cloth to cover it. He said he hadn't got a cloth, but that the steam would stay in the bucket if I ran with it to the fitter's workshop. I did, but surprise, surprise, there was no steam left in the bucket by the time I got to the workshop a mere twenty feet away! I displayed this kind of naïveté a few times before I copped on.

One of my jobs was to clean the canteen and later on the games room. The lads used to leave their unfinished lunches behind and I would eat some of them, because I frequently left home without any breakfast or lunch and had no money to get anything from the shops, having spent the little I had over the previous weekend, or having loaned it to my mother. This was only one step up from the times when I picked sweets up from the ground on my way to and from school because I had no money at all and it was better than going hungry.

At this stage, I was making my first tentative attempts at dating, without much success it has to be said. I met a girl in Weavex and fell head over heels for her. I was irrepressible in my efforts to get her to go out on a date with me, but it was to no avail, though we did become friends and I got to visit her at her home on Ballyfermot Road. I would find out what music she liked and I would make sure to bring along her favourite singers, Glen Campbell, the New Seekers and The Stylistics. One of her all-time favourite songs was, 'Honey

Come Back', and I tried to woo her by singing it at the top of my voice, much to her chagrin. I still blush thinking about it.

For some time I had fancied that I would write a song. She inspired me to do just that. I can't remember them now, but there were quite a few and they were very intense. It was much later that I figured out that I had been writing the kinds of songs that I would have wanted someone to write for me. Alas, she remained unimpressed at my gallant efforts. But she couldn't put me off and for years I wanted to date her more than any other girl I knew.

At a dinner dance at the Fitzpatrick Hotel in Portmarnock, she looked beautiful in her cream floral dress and my heart melted at the sight of her, but she would not dance with me, much to my frustration and disappointment. I have such strong memories of that night and of the Chicago song: 'If you Leave me Now', as I felt that she was not to be mine. She had left Weavex shortly before this event and it was to be the last time I saw her for another two years, and in the most unexpected place.

I loved to sing and I did plenty of it while working in Weavex. The lads on the night shift would ask me to sing for them whenever I was working late. My favourite song at that time was 'Power to All our Friends' by Cliff Richard and 'Red, Red Wine' sung by Neil Diamond. When I sang 'Power to All our Friends', I did the same actions to the song that Cliff had done in the Eurovision Song Contest. I would stretch my arm into the air while bringing my knees together. The guys loved it and found it very entertaining.

However, as much fun as we had at work, bullying was frequent. One very hot summer's day in 1976, another worker and I were working extremely hard unloading and loading a forty-foot container in sweltering heat. No surprise then that we were sweating like the proverbial pigs. When we needed to take a break, we went in behind the sewing machines where it was nice and cool. The next thing we heard, a girl called out to the supervisor at the top of her voice: 'Girls, can you get a terrible smell? Jean, Jean there's a terrible smell over here.'

The supervisor came over and started to sniff in an exaggerated fashion. She then came over to where we were standing and proceeded to sniff me from head to toe. 'Jaysus, you smell like a smelly dog. Stay there until I come back.' She went up to her office and returned with a bottle of perfume and proceeded to spray it all over me. 'Now,' she said, 'that's much better'.

The months and years passed, until I reached the age of seventeen. I had been promoted to the position of auxiliary weaver, but was still stuck in the packing and dispatch department. Then, I was approached by the production manager at about 8.30 on a Monday morning.

'Thomas, what age are you now?' I replied that I was seventeen.

'Then would you be interested in training to be a weaver?' I couldn't believe it. Of course, I accepted immediately, especially as it meant leaving the packing and despatch department for good. It also meant a significant increase in my wages, which delighted me, especially as I thought it would please my mother. She seemed indifferent to my news and when I asked for a pay increase she told me I could have an extra £1! I was so disappointed and angry, especially as around this time, I learned that my other brothers were handing up a great deal less then me.

What made this even more unfair was the fact that I was earning far more than any of them and worked very long hours to do so. I was determined to rectify this situation and bided my time. A few months after starting my training I started shift work, which meant another significant wage increase and left me as the biggest earner in the family, but still, after I had handed my wages over, I was the lowest paid. The only good thing about all of this was that it meant being away from the house more, especially with my other work on behalf of the Peace Corps.

But no matter how much I had appreciated the promotion there was always going to be one major downside; I wasn't able to have my conversations with the girls and I did miss them a lot. I thoroughly detested the manner in which the men spoke to the women or spoke about them behind their backs. I was mortified by the pictures of nude girls in the *Mirror* and the *Sun* and the calendars on display in the maintenance workshop.

One of the most embarrassing experiences of this period was when one of the weavers asked me if I ever had wet dreams. I had heard about them but wasn't sure what they were, so, rather than display total ignorance, I replied that, 'I do wake up sweating sometimes!' That was a cause of great mirth as was my speech impediment — I had a lisp. I would be in the canteen or the rest room when some one or other of them would say, 'Thomas, say "chlicken and clchips".' There was no malice in it, though it was embarrassing. Many years later I was to regret losing my lisp after being told that it made me sound very feminine; just another of those ironies, I suppose.

The experience of the wet dreams made me more determined than ever to pin my parents down and get them to tell me the facts of life. I went home from work having spent the day preoccupied with how I was going to broach the subject with them. I decided to ask straight out: 'Mam, would you please tell me the facts of life? I'm seventeen now and still don't have a clue, and it's getting embarrassing with the fellas at work asking me questions about wet dreams and stuff. And I still don't know how to ask girls out.'

She just told me to speak to my father, that he was in the shed and that it would be the ideal time to catch him, especially as he was in a good mood. So off up the garden path I went towards the shed, with my stomach in knots, and asked Dad the same question. And now I was to receive my father's wisdom on women and how to treat them: 'There are just two things you need to know about women. First, make sure you never get VD, and two, make sure you never get into a joint bank account with a woman.'

That's it? I thought. I was dumbfounded. With my ever-growing sense of detachment from being a male, I couldn't relate to what he just told me, particularly given my innate dislike for being a man to begin with. There was, though, the final awful realisation that this was not a man in whom I could ever confide, who unashamedly stated that men who molested women and abused children should be castrated and yet who would prove guilty of that very sin himself. Hypocrisy, it seemed, was to be the norm in adult morality.

Chapter 4

Puberty: Knowing I'm Different

Heavenly hurt, it gives us —
We can find no scar,
But internal difference,
Where the meanings are.
[EMILY DICKINSON]

There was nothing on my body that would ever let you think I was a girl, except maybe the missing Adam's apple. There were no scars that would in any way indicate that I was wounded and there was nothing on the outside to show that I was in the most excruciating mental and emotional conflict, but I was and it really did hurt. Heaven knew and did nothing, at least that's what I thought until fairly recently. Now, I realise and accept that this simply is not true. Heaven did indeed have its purpose, but waited a lifetime to reveal it, and all the while I had to cope with being different, very different.

Puberty and adolescence can be traumatic at the best of times, but going through adolescence with a conflicting gender identity is so much worse. It is very difficult for most of us to admit to being confused about sexual matters while we go through this phase in our development, but the constant uncertainty surrounding who I was, and now am, made it extremely difficult to know my sexual orientation and it was to be many years before I was to understand the complex process I was going through. I had a growing awareness of being alienated from my own body and at times even from my own mind. I became increasingly conscious of being double-minded, or double-gendered in the way I viewed the world around me. My obvious preference for female company and friendship was becoming much more pronounced and causing me no end of problems socially.

It never really occurred to me that I was wrong to expect to grow breasts and to have my periods along with every other girl. I genuinely believed that I was sooner or later going to start entering into womanhood with a body to match how I was feeling inside. But as time went on and the wrong parts started to grow and expand, then I truly did freak out, albeit internally. I was absolutely terrified by what was happening and could only scream back into my own being because it was simply impossible to explain this to anyone else, and I do mean anyone. Had I done so then I am absolutely certain I would have been put into a psychiatric ward.

I was utterly certain that I was living and dying in the wrong body; that instead of having a penis I should have had a vagina and that instead of having a flat chest, I should have had breasts. How was I to explain just how freaked out I was at having facial hair and chest hair, when I knew I should not have had either. I became obsessive in comparing myself to other girls, wondering if, just maybe, things would suddenly change, that the dreadful mistake would finally be realised and that my body would be put right of its own accord. But it never did and I was left to obsess and fantasise about how my life might have been had my body developed as it was supposed to.

I wondered how on earth girls could complain so much about their periods when, to me, it was one of the greatest affirmations of their womanhood. I cried at the thought, and grieved over it and the fact that I would never have that experience; that I would never get to complain about my own periods, to take them for granted and feel so complete and so completely normal. I, Sara, lost my own right to live as I should; as a beautiful teenage girl sharing all the same apprehensions about entering womanhood with all my teenage girl friends. It just never happened for me.

It is only now that I have researched my condition that I understand why my body didn't do what I had always expected, and indeed longed, for it to do. Mine was a male body containing a female gender identity and the two were completely irreconcilable. Although there were still some indicators that things should have been different. For example not having an Adam's apple; my voice being very soft, along with my hands and getting pimples around my face and mouth regularly on a monthly basis, which I was later to learn was female acne. I was often questioned about why my hands were so soft and feminine looking, despite them being large and used to the same hard work as the guys I worked with. Then there was my distinctly feminine posture and hand movements, which, though I tried desperately to hide them over the years, were still spotted by some and even raised some questions about my sexuality. Looking back, there was outside evidence even then that my body was not as it should be.

Just like any teenager, I became more naturally inclined to worry about my body and personal appearance, but some of my interests and concerns regarding my clothes, personal hygiene and social interactions were becoming decidedly more feminine, but because I was afraid of being called a 'cissy', I became quite adept at hiding some of my instinctively feminine traits, especially my body language and deportment.

The most marked development at this time was in my emotions and communications. My emotional development was definitely shifting more towards the feminine rather than masculine. It was also during my teens that I began to experience what can best be described as out-of-body experiences and became more detached and divided from myself. There was a little girl inside screaming from within my own body, trying desperately to fight her way out of years of conforming to my male upbringing. But there was no giving up this time and, despite the many long years it was to take Sara to claim her right to live; she, I, was determined to assert my natural birthright, regardless of how I looked on the outside. But for the time being, it would be more about skirmishes rather than full-blown battles. Winning the battles was still a long way off.

I had very few opportunities, if any, to dress during my teens and that caused me much distress. The truth is that I felt like a complete freak living in a boy's body. Others never noticed, due to my ability to *act* the teenage boy, but I certainly felt that there was nothing about me that fit into the society in which I was raised.

As I watched all these changes in my body and realised that there was nothing I could do about them, I became terribly sad and depressed. I felt completely helpless, with not a single soul to turn to. The best I could hope for was that it would in some miraculous way change of its own accord; of course it never did. So, I tried to deal with it as best I could and spent a lot of time making sure I was properly groomed, especially when attending social occasions. It is ironic that this was the one thing about which my mother was most complimentary!

There is no getting away from the fact that I felt utterly cheated, but helpless to do anything about my situation. This was made so much worse by not being able to tell anyone about what I was going through. It was bad enough that I was already being bullied for being left-handed, tall, for reading books, and working with the Peace Corps and for being 'retarded'. So, imagine my difficulty even thinking about the fact that I felt I was a girl living in a boy's body! It just didn't bear thinking about, and so I really tried not to and just got on with being the best teenage *boy* that I could be. It didn't work.

It was during my early teens — thirteen to fourteen, to be precise, that I first bought my own clothes. I remember my first ever suit, which I bought in Weavers to Wearer in Henry Street. Even from that age I loved shopping, even if it meant getting into debt to do it. My mother's response to my complaints about my low wages was to give me 'credit notes', which took the urgency out of giving me a proper wage.

The downside to shopping was that I couldn't go to the boutiques, which was where I really wanted to shop. It was the greatest strain trying to walk past all those beautiful clothes and shoes. Sometimes, I was mentally exhausted from the effort.

I tried to find a way to buy clothes that would look and feel feminine but would not give the game away, so I bought orange, pink and purple round-collared shirts and flared pants with stripes running down the legs. I even tried to buy unisex nylon underwear that at least looked like it could be worn by girls.

Nonetheless, despite my best efforts, I was unable to act in the same way as my brothers and other boys my age. For example, I simply could not identify in any way with the manner in which boys treated girls, especially their vulgarity and rudeness; the way they would speak of 'touching them up' and 'dropping the hand'. Just listening to them made me sick, and it didn't go unnoticed. At least some of my brothers and sisters were curious about this, and reminded me of this after hearing of my later diagnosis. They were also curious about my difficulties in chatting up girls and the way that I became increasingly withdrawn. Some of them called me a cissy and some wanted to know if I was 'queer'. Interestingly, they would also attribute my search for spiritual answers as a search for my true self. Strange how they could recognise this truth, yet treat me so badly at the same time.

I was particularly revolted by the way they spoke about girls having their periods and referring to them as having their 'flowers'. If a girl did not want to dance or go on a date she would be called a 'homo' or a 'lezzer'! And if she was having a bad day she was said to be 'in her rags'. These were common insults used against girls who spoke up for them- selves or who were having a bad time. Other comments would be made about girls developing breasts.

My own brothers teased my sisters quite a bit and it made me extremely angry, though whenever I spoke out against them speaking that way, they, along with my mother, would tell me to shut up and mind my own business. But there can be no doubt that these comments did hurt my sisters, despite their best efforts to laugh them off. Some of them admitted as much to me years later.

I really did identify with them but was completely excluded from their company, especially when they were hanging out together. I so wanted to be a part of their group. I was very tuned into my sisters' feelings whenever they were having boyfriend problems and some of them would confide in me, one sister in particular. And yet we never really became close. This was impossible given their need to be accepted by their mother, and it was her disapproval of me that, I believe, ensured we would never be close. This remains one of the greatest sadnesses of my life. Whatever about the estrangement I feel from my brothers, not having a relationship with my sisters is infinitely worse; at times I would love to share things with them, or to be able to meet up for coffee or lunch.

It was also during my teens that I decided to do something about my lack of education and the fact that I was semi-literate at best. It had bothered me for such a long time that I wasn't allowed to finish school and that I could barely read or write. I determined to prove to the people who had branded me a retard and stupid that I was just as normal as they were. This has been the second dominant motivation of my life apart from trying to allow Sara the right to live as nature intended. It was a huge mountain to climb but I was determined to climb it. I was resolved to teach myself to read and write and embarked on a journey that I've been on ever since. I love learning new things, new words, new insights; anything that enhances my understanding of life and the world around me.

Because I felt I was so far behind everyone else, I thought I would have to read books at a much higher level than primary school, so I started to buy books that were at university level. This filled me with trepidation but I was convinced that there was no other option. Along with reading was the need to have good handwriting, so I practised my handwriting every day and looked for reasons to write things down, especially taking notes and writing letters. I got down to some serious reading with books on psychology, sociology, history etc. It was really hard but I was determined. No sooner had I started reading, than I realised I had a very poor vocabulary and that I wasn't making much progress because I wasn't able to understand a lot of the words I was reading, so I bought my first ever dictionary and thesaurus. Every time I came to a word I could not understand, I would go to the dictionary and, once I found the correct definition, would write it in the margin of the book and run a line under the sentence so that I could refer to it whenever that word occurred elsewhere in the book. This is how I learned the importance of under-standing things in their context. I would then use the words I had learnt in my everyday conversation. Once I got the hang of reading, I then started to develop a love for studying and learning new things and it has been one of my passions ever since.

I began to expand my reading interests and started to read more literature and developed a great liking for period dramas and documentaries and later in my teens I developed a love of classical music. This was a very unusual thing for someone my age to do, but it never occurred to me at the time and was another of the reasons offered by my siblings for finding me 'weird'. I was damned if I wasn't educated and damned if I was; a no-win situation. But it has held me in good stead ever since. Being self-educated went a long way towards helping me to become a good conversationalist and a good socialiser. Burying myself in learning and music helped me to suppress my conflict with my gender identity even further, but not so much that I could hide my very girl-like emotions, especially my crying at romantic films and sad situations.

By now, it was 1976 and I was sixteen years old, desperate to escape from my pain, feeling misunderstood by my family and colleagues, and increasingly disconnected from my true self. My life had barely even started and I now began to think about trying to end it. I felt that I didn't belong to anyone and I didn't belong anywhere. I felt as if I was staring into a hole and seeing nothing but perpetual darkness. The most obvious thing to do, it seemed, was to remove myself from this life, and from being the inconvenience my family seemed to feel me to be. So I tried. One night, I went to the canal bridge on the Kylemore Road. I hauled myself up onto the railing over the canal, and leaned over, staring into the black water below. All I needed to do was to jump. I was just seconds away from that final leap of faith, when something stopped me. It suddenly occurred to me that there might be another way. It was a long shot, but it might just work. What if I left home and changed my name, so I couldn't be found? The very thought of it was enough to make me change my mind. Yes, that's what I'll do, I thought. I'll leave home and change my name. I didn't know how to do either, but at that pivotal moment it was enough to give me a reason to go on living.

Having made that decision, I immediately tried to imagine a life away from my family and how best to achieve this. The idea alone gave me some sense of control over my life — a feeling I had never had until this time. It felt truly liberating. I walked away from the canal bridge that night with an overwhelming sense of joy and determination, resolved to find a more purposeful way of escaping the terrible situation I had been bound to for so many years. It was a fateful decision for another reason, too. I was so focused on breaking free of my family that I didn't really deal with the issue that would impact on my life even more: my conflicting gender identity. At the time, I believed that my 'strange feelings' were due to the situation with my family. So it made sense to me to believe that, if I got away from them, my other problem would eventually resolve itself. It didn't.

My attempt to break free from my family failed. I tried to find a place to stay but was unsuccessful. I tried the Salvation Army, across from the Royal College of Surgeons and Sarsfield House, but was found unsuitable, so I had to stay put and to find other ways of escaping. After that, my work became my great escape and the FCA and religion, and I threw myself into these with single-minded focus. Ultimately, I did what I was expected to do or thought I was expected to do and that was, find a nice girl, settle down and start a family.

*

At seventeen I joined the FCA and stayed there for eighteen months. I felt that it was the 'right' thing to do to normalise my life and to help me fit in. In truth, I enjoyed the experience and felt I was serving my country in some way. I was not myself whenever I wore that uniform, and it was a time when I felt respected by others. But I did win the prize for best-dressed soldier several times! Although we were supposed to wear our trousers tucked into our boots, I wore mine over the top of my boots, as I thought it looked nicer.

I joined the 11th Motor Squadron in McKee Barracks and was in Troop 3; Trooper Thomas Dunne. On the night I signed up I was under age by a few months. I never let on that my father was one of their colleagues and that he had served with them over the years. I hated name-dropping and wanted to get by on my own merits. I attended barracks every Thursday night and learned how to use various kinds of weapons, including the Lee-Enfield, the FN and the Gustav. All the weapons were designed for right-handers and, being left-handed, I found it difficult to use some of them, which was a cause of great merriment when I was on the firing range during shooting practice. Some of the officers took bets that I would either not be able to hit my targets or would score very low. In fact, I consistently had above-average scores and in the Gustav practice, I scored the second-highest on the day. Quite an achievement for a left-hander!

We would go on camps to the Glen of Imaal and Gormanstown. And in the summer we went on an annual camp to Longford. I was assigned to work with the cook, who just happened to have a major gripe against the officers because they had lost his discharge papers. He clearly did not believe them and so carried a grudge against them, which he exercised against them on a daily basis, without their ever knowing about it. When he was cooking for the officers, he would take their steaks, throw them on the floor and wipe them across the floor with a filthy mop. He would leave the vegetables in the cupboard to go off for several days before using them and with great relish he would spit phlegm into the teapot. It was utterly disgusting and I didn't know what to say or do about it.

It was while in Longford that the photograph was taken of
me sucking my thumb. I had returned early from a night out
at a local pub and had fallen asleep early. The lads came back
and found me asleep and sucking my thumb. It was to be
another four years before I finally managed to overcome the
habit. Sucking my thumb was the only comforter I had when
distressed. There was nowhere and no-one to turn to for
comfort so I went to sleep sucking my thumb.

I requested a discharge from the FCA after I had made my
decision to sign up for the priesthood in 1978, but not before
I had learned of my being promoted to an NCO. I'd requested
my discharge before going onto the NCOs course as I felt that
staying with the army was incompatible with preparing for
the priesthood and my ongoing commitment to the Peace
Corps, which I was still involved with during my time with
the FCA. They granted my request and I left the FCA in the
autumn of 1978. Just weeks before my Nan died.

I had finished my night shift in Weavex and had gone to bed,
but I was awoken from my sleep to the sounds of my sisters'
screams: 'Nana is dead, Nana is dead!' Nan had just died and
my sisters' words were pounding in my head. I got dressed
and went straight down to see Nan. I'd wished I hadn't. What
I saw horrified me. She was lying in my uncle's arms, her eyes
staring in terror at her impending death. My mother had
always told us how terrified she was of dying.

That night we held the wake and I stayed up all night looking after my uncles. My uncle Seamus refused to go and see
his mother and had to be coaxed up by my other uncles. I
told him that he would probably always regret it if he didn't
go up and that it would probably prevent him from getting
closure later on. He eventually went up to see her and, as

expected, he fell to pieces. It was strange to see the same uncle who had spat on the ground and said: 'my mother isn't worth that spit to me' now grieving. It was a shocking experience and brought home to me that there were others who were prepared to be brutally honest about their feelings towards their mothers. This was a major taboo at that time, and still is, to a large extent.

My uncles asked me to sing during the wake in honour of Nan. They told me how much she loved me and that I was one of her favourites and of how she enjoyed my visits late at night on my way home from my work with the Peace Corps. She also appreciated my bringing her bottles of stout and Gold Bond cigarettes. She especially appreciated that I continuously ran the gauntlet of my mother's fury, defying her insistence that I keep away from Nan. I don't know what happened between Nan and my mother, beyond my nan calling my father a 'bastard'. But it was enough to leave my mother feeling embittered towards her until just before her death when something changed and brought them to some form of reconciliation.

They reminded me that Nan thought of me as that 'lovable little fucker', as she had called me just a few months earlier. My nan was my oasis, I could confide in her without fear of things ever getting back to my mother, and, whereas my mother seemed to hate the sight of me, my nan was always delighted to see me. She was the only one I felt I could truly trust.

On the following night Nan was removed from the house to the church of the Assumption. We walked behind her coffin. The next day was the funeral mass and she was later buried in St Fintan's Cemetery in Howth, near where she once lived. It was extremely hard saying goodbye to my only ally.

By the time I'd left my teens behind I had developed a very intense personality and was strongly committed to whatever it was I believed in. I was also very loyal to those I cared about and who showed kindness towards me. And I'd already learned the importance of a well-rounded education, coupled with an open mind and tolerance towards those who happened to be different. And why would it be any other way, because who knew more about what it meant to be different than a young woman living in the body of a young man?

That was how life was to be for me, during the 70s. Busy, busy and even more busy; that was how I drowned out the sound of Sara's cries for help and how I tried to rid myself of those ever-present nightmares of her being buried alive. I had joined the Peace Corps when I was seventeen and then the local folk group. We sang at twelve o'clock Mass every Sunday and for the patients at the Cheshire Home in the Phoenix Park. Every year we held our peace concerts. They were always a sell-out and extremely enjoyable. Folk group practice was every Thursday evening in the Dominican girls' school. I also worked for Welfare Action, an organisation dedicated to helping the poor, a couple of nights a week, as I liked the idea of helping others less fortunate than myself. We visited peoples' homes to do painting and decorating, shopping, gardening etc. We also arranged delivery of goods donated by members of the public to poorer families, which could be televisions, furniture etc. I later became the leader of the local Welfare Action group, and later still became the coordinator of the Welfare Cadets, which was established in May 1978.

Ever since surviving my first suicide attempt and my ever-growing desire to get away from my family, I found that my job and voluntary work gave me great solace. But nothing could compensate for my sense of loss at not being my true self. It is fair to say that my alienation from my family was copper-fastened during this period, as was my alienation from Sara. What I didn't really appreciate then was just how much of a weirdo my family considered me to be, especially because of my helping others. They simply could not understand why I would join the Peace Corps and be such an intellectual. They were forever slagging me off, because of my vocabulary and my taste in clothes and music. They let on not to like my taste in music, while playing my records behind my back and wearing my clothes out on their dates, all the while saying that I could not accompany them to dances in the TV Club and the Apartment. I was cramping their style and I was too boring, they said. It is entirely true that I was not the best of company when out with them. This was because I was finding it increasingly difficult to converse with my peers as a boy, when all I felt inside was this girl wanting to find expression.

It was during this period that I began to be excluded from an increasing number of family functions. My mother and one brother in particular made sure that I was excluded. Every time an invitation was issued for some function or other, this brother would say, 'I'm not going if Thomas is going'. To which request my mother always acceded, while pretending to do her best to change his mind. She never did and the reason was increasingly clear; he was the undoubted favourite. Everyone towed the line and ignored me at every opportunity; so much so that when their own birthdays or other celebrations came up, I was either completely excluded or given a token invitation, in the hope that I would refrain from attending. I was getting the message and so found reasons not to attend, but this never stopped me from helping them whenever they needed me, and need me they did.

Happiness is not a word I would have used to describe any stage in my life prior to my going public about my condition. Were there times when I was happy? Of course, but they were so intermittent and too often accompanied by an immediate sense of dread as to render them difficult to remember. There were those special moments when I discovered a beautiful piece of music or heard a song that went straight to my heart, or the times when I did well at something and had it acknowledged, but they were in all truthfulness, few and far between.

I would go for long walks through the fields off Le Fanu Road and up and down Ballyfermot Road; going to the church in order to pray for direction and to be able to make some sense of my life and my family's treatment of me, for reasons I couldn't fathom. These were just some of the ways in which I tried to get time for myself and connect with God in order to get answers to my questions. But the divine was always too abstract and inaccessible, I felt, a remote power but with great control over our minds and spirits.

I tried to find God directly through my own prayers; never able to understand why such an intelligent God would have me pray to him in mindless repetitions. Of course, I was to discover later on that he doesn't want us to use mindless scripted prayers, chants or mantras. He wants us to talk to him intelligently. But that was for later on, for now I had to be content with asking questions about why He had allowed me to go through so much turmoil. Of course, I didn't know that, even as I was going through my own difficulties, my sisters were also going through their own traumas; something I could never have imagined possible.

Some of my greatest fun moments at this time were the Peace Corps' trips to Glencree. I went on quite a few of them and always enjoyed them immensely. We also travelled up to Corrymeela on the Antrim Coast, near Giant's Causeway. These trips were part of the North-South exchange, in which we were attempting to get a better understanding of the different cultures and their feelings about the Troubles. At the time, there wasn't a day or week went by without a bomb going off or someone being murdered. Then there was the massacres, such as the Miami Showband. There were moments during this period when I thought the world was going to end, such was the darkness of the clouds that hung over this country. It was hoped that these meetings would help to create a common understanding and tolerance towards each other and that this would help towards a more peaceful society within Northern Ireland; or as we called it, the North. It was quite an experience driving through the border checkpoints and seeing all the British soldiers and their weapons and armoured vehicles, a mixture of awe and fear.

I was coming towards the end of my teens and with it came an intensity of mind and a vacant heart. Sara had been abandoned in favour of 'fitting in'. Everything she was and could have been had been smothered and it seemed for the most part that she was gone for good. The nameless teenager entering womanhood with all her desire for life and all that that should have been, was buried alive and for the most part forgotten. However, Sara may have been sent to limbo, but she was not for staying there.

Over the coming years, Sara would find her own way of defying Thomas's suppression and though it was very secretive, it did allow her to give some defiant expression of her right to *be*. Sara and Thomas had begun a countdown towards ultimate separation and Sara claiming her right to life. But what was to become of Thomas? Only time would tell.

Chapter 5
Dating

Love has the power of making you believe what
you normally treat with the utmost suspicion
[MIRABEAU]

I know of men and women who have married rather than admit to being gay and in many cases have entered the religious life for the same reason. In my case, I dated because I wanted to be normal, not because I was gay, lesbian or bi-sexual. (Gender identity disorder is not to be confused with sexual orientation: there are differing sexual orientations in GID and non-GID people.) I came through this whole period without any conclusive answers regarding my sexuality. It was to be one of the least concerns for me during this whole period and for the most part this remains the case. At the time, I simply felt a desperate need to be loved and to live a normal life.

I was at least seventeen before I managed to get a date, which by the standards set by my brothers, made me a late starter. My brothers had been dating at a much earlier age and they were beginning to wonder about me, not that they were any help. I was absolutely hopeless with chat-up lines and couldn't ask a girl out to save my life. I was far more interested in good conversation than chatting up girls, which, under the circumstances, should come as no surprise. I'm sure it must have made me very boring but I simply never got the 'chatting-up' bit.

When I was dating I found it extremely difficult to think of girls sexually and I found it equally difficult listening to boys talk about them in that way; and yet, at the same time, I wasn't attracted to boys either. For me, friendship was always far more important with girls than anything else and I found myself able to love them in that way; most probably because I was overwhelmed at the mere thought of having a girl-friend as opposed to a girl friend. This led me to get carried away at times, coming on too strong. Try as I might to get it right, I was simply incapable of being a competent dater, and this was to show itself in so many ways; not the least being my inability to draw a clear line between being a 'boy' dating 'girls'. I wanted to talk about girls' things and not the things boys would talk about, which I'm certain must have been very disconcerting for the girls I dated.

I remember doing a Personal Development course in Newcastle West in 1998, and on the course many of the women were surprised at how much I knew about women and about *being* a woman. But they were also extremely doubtful when I told them I'd never made a single pass at a woman (maybe they'll believe it now!) and that I always felt extremely uncomfortable having to be the one to ask women out on a date. I told them I never once used a chat-up line on a woman, which again they refused to believe. And of course, why wouldn't they, after all they saw me as a man and not as a woman. Looking back, these encounters, which grew in number and frequency over the years, were to become my unconscious way of trying to integrate as a woman, despite my best efforts to consciously suppress my feminine traits.

Given the choice between my male colleagues at work and my female colleagues, I much preferred the females. If I had to choose between talking about sports, cars, machines, war films etc. on the one hand, and relationships, children, fashion, makeup, socialising, with girls on the other, then there was no competition. I would certainly opt for the latter. But of course I was stuck trying to fit in with my male colleagues, which I found intolerable. Nonetheless, I did try my very best to fit in and to prove I was as normal as everyone else during this period and beyond.

My attempts were frustrated by the fact that I was getting absolutely no feedback from anyone. I can well understand why people would have felt confused about where I was coming from and what my motives might have been, as I was experiencing so much confusion myself and was desperately trying to come up with answers that would set me on the path to 'normality'. This was especially a problem with my efforts at trying to determine my sexuality; something I still feel uncomfortable dealing with. The best way I can describe it is that I am sexually ambiguous and that it is not a major issue in my life. However, none of these realisations were to be of any help to me during my teens and even during my twenties and thirties.

When I eventually managed to get a date I really wish I hadn't. The girl I asked out was a member of the Peace Corps. It was my brother's 21st birthday party. It was due to be held in the Green Isle Hotel on the Naas Road. I asked a girl on a normal date first but she turned me down, so I resorted to impressing her by inviting her to my brother's party. I decided to pluck up the courage to ask her during the week of our peace concerts in the Dominican Covent. She turned me down flat, but I wasn't giving up that easily. It just so happened that my eldest brother was having an engagement dinner in the Green Isle Hotel, so I asked the girl a second time if she would go out with me to the Green Isle, and this time she agreed. But the dinner was cancelled for reasons I can't remember, so I had to come up with a plan B. I told her I would take her to the La Dolce Vita club in Mary Street. It was a new club that was *the* place to go.

I was all dressed up in my best and full of excitement at the prospect of having a nice date. However, when we arrived at La Dolce Vita we were refused entry on account of us not being members. I suspect that the real reason was that we were both under age, but the doorman was very discreet and clearly didn't want to embarrass me in front of her. The problem for now was that I didn't have a plan C! But she came to the rescue by suggesting that we go and see *Gone with the Wind*. I was only too happy to agree and so we went. While we were watching the film, I did the usual boy thing of trying to put my arm around her shoulder. I was so slow about it that I made snails look like sprinters. When I finally managed to get to the other side she was completely unresponsive so I discreetly removed it while I cringed inside.

During the intermission, she asked me go buy her 20 Rothmans and I duly obliged, in spite of having to leave the cinema and go across the road to get them. As I passed the ladies' toilets I saw her with her sister and her friend giggling and when they saw me they quickly re-entered the toilet and closed the door. It took her ages to return to her seat and when she did, it was obvious that she wasn't at all interested in the date. I brought her home and when we got to the gate I asked her if she would let me know. She gave me a kiss on the cheek and that was the last date I had with her.

I had much greater success, and was to make a firm friend, with my third date. Small and bubbly, she had joined the Welfare Cadets some months earlier and really seemed to enjoy working with me. She was very enthusiastic and committed. She was also much fancied by many of the guys and they were forever trying to chat her up, but to no avail.

The Peace Corps, who were associated with the Welfare Cadets, were having one of their many nights out bowling in Stillorgan and I invited her along as it would be an opportunity for her to socialise with the Peace Corps, which she was keen to join. We were all waiting at the bus stop outside Trinity College when it started to rain. The bus was at the stop and the driver sat there and wouldn't let us get on, in spite of the fact that it was pouring rain. I thought that he was being stupid and inconsiderate and so took it upon myself to open the door and let everyone on. The driver refused to allow me to get on so they all left for the bowling without me. She decided to get off the bus too, which surprised me greatly. She said that if I wasn't going, then neither was she. I was absolutely delighted with myself, as I fancied her like mad. The problem was, I didn't have any other plan. She suggested we go to the pictures, so we decided to go and see *Saturday Night Fever* in the Savoy. It was wonderful. As we sat there watching the film I plucked up the courage to put my arm around her shoulders. She was very responsive and the feeling was truly electrifying. I was way above the proverbial cloud nine. So much so that I ventured to kiss her, and again she was receptive. I can hardly describe just how completely wonderful she made me feel; words cannot do it justice.

Of course, I had to spoil it by telling her some time later that I loved her. I allowed myself to get completely carried away and scared the living daylights out of her with my intense feelings. She was, after all, just fifteen and I was just seventeen.

Convincing myself that I wasn't meant to date girls and that I should once again consider my vocation, I did so over a period of weeks until I finally resolved to apply for the priesthood and went to see the Director of Vocations, Consular Brennan, at Ringsend in April 1978. I spent about two hours with him, going through all the reasons why I thought I had a vocation. He was convinced that I had and so got me to fill in this enormous form. I signed it and, in signing it, agreed to attend the local VEC for two years in order to get a formal education, which was absolutely vital if I was to study at Clonliffe College.

Once I had made my decision, I decided to tell my parents. My mother was delighted and said she would do everything she could to help me, including getting a job if necessary. For the first time ever I thought she was proud of me. And why wouldn't she be, thinking I was eventually going to be the first in the family to join the priesthood, a huge thing in those days. A family's prestige increased greatly after the ordination of one of its own. Once I had told my family, I felt my resolve grow even stronger and so began preparing myself in every way I could while waiting for the school year to begin.

It was at this time that I told my girlfriend of my decision to train for the priesthood. I could see that she had very mixed feelings about it. On the one hand there was an obvious disappointment and on the other, she said that she was pleased for me and would help me in any way she could, and she did. On my eighteenth birthday she bought me a Bible. It was a Roman Catholic Revised Standard Version and carried the *Imprimatur* and *Nihil Obstat*. This was to be crucially important for me later, when confronting some very difficult discoveries I would make, subsequent to my reading this particular version of the Bible.

These discoveries, to do with celibacy and the grounds for divorce, the Catholic Bible's version of which I disagreed with, gave me a determination to withdraw my application to Clonliffe College and later still, formally to resign from the Roman Catholic Church, much to the chagrin of my parents, even though they were not practising Catholics themselves. Immensely difficult though the decision may have been, it is one I have never lived to regret.

Hardly had I made the decision not to go ahead and join the priesthood than I met Barbara, my future wife. It was this fateful meeting that was to overshadow my struggle with my gender conflict for the next twenty years.

Chapter 6
A Fatal Marriage

Many marriages are first announced, then
denounced and finally renounced
[ANONYMOUS]

Call me an idealist, call me a romantic, call me naïve, but I really do believe in love; so much so that I could never contemplate living without it, or at least the hope of finding it. And this despite the many hurts that loving can bring. The problem was, I was so desperate to find love, or what appeared to be love, that I allowed myself to enter into a disastrous relationship and an even more disastrous marriage.

I met Barbara in the autumn of 1978. I was coming down Ballyfermot Road one evening after a night spent on Peace Corps' work. I had just made my decision not to go ahead and study for the priesthood and it was only days after my nan had died. I passed two girls by and one of them called after me, saying, 'Don't say hello then'. I had met Barbara a couple of times on the street, but had never got further than 'hello'. That night, I went back to her and we started chatting. She said goodnight to her friend and I walked her to her gate. I plucked up the courage to ask her out on a date. To my amazement, she said yes, so we arranged to meet the following Thursday.

I was like a giddy child going home, hardly able to believe my luck. I spent the next week between a state of delight and utter mortification. Delight at having a date, dread at the fact that I couldn't actually remember her name. I was hoping that she might answer the door herself — if one of her family answered, then I was going to be in a right pickle. I would have to say something like, 'Hi, I'm here to see the girl with the glasses.' I still get embarrassed thinking about it.

Thankfully, one of Barbara's friends came to the rescue. I bumped into her on the way to Barbara's house and, when I told her about my predicament, she very kindly offered to go to the door for me — though not without having a good laugh first.

The first date amounted to nothing more than going for a walk, chatting and a kiss goodnight. We arranged to meet and go to the pictures the following Sunday. I arrived for our date only to find Barbara house-sitting, looking after her grandparents. Both her parents were out, as were her three sisters and two brothers. When her grandparents eventually left, we sat and looked at the *Muppet Show*, amongst other things. About 10.30 p.m. her father came in. We were sitting in the dark, so he couldn't see me. The first words out of his mouth were, 'Is that that long bastard?' I was shocked and rooted to the sofa, but Barbara was quick to reassure me that her father was not referring to me, but instead to her ex-boyfriend. Needless to say, his arrival and abrupt tone put an early end to proceedings.

Barbara gave me my first, and very nearly my last, Christmas present some weeks later, a silver chain and medallion with my name engraved on it. No sooner did she hand it to me, then she told me she was calling it off. I was devastated and didn't know what to do. I cried my eyes out. I was distraught. She was shocked by my reaction. I pleaded with her to tell me why. She said that she did not think it would work out. I told her I loved her and that I didn't want to finish with her. Then, as cool as you like she said, 'Actually, I was just testing you.' I was too relieved to be annoyed. This was to prove the first of many *tests* she was to put me through.

Nonetheless, as I was desperate for love and support, I stuck with it.

We began to see each other virtually every night. She brought me to stay with her sister Lily and her family in Tallaght after just two weeks. While there I met Lily's two children, Aaron and Linda. We went to the Waldorf in the city centre for some drinks and dancing. When we came back we were given the sofa bed to share. We stayed up most of the night, and around three in the morning, I proposed to her, and to my surprise and delight, she accepted. I was astonished because I never really believed that anyone would actually love me, never mind marry me. So I took the first chance I got. How foolish and immature I was.

Being brutally honest about it, I have always felt much more comfortable having women as friends rather than lovers. I have loved them but more as companions than as prospective wives and, though I'd asked Barbara to marry me, I was still extremely uncomfortable with taking the initiative, especially when it came to matters sexual, but that is what I was expected to do and I had enough problems without people thinking I might be gay. The great issue for me was one of surviving my family and my relationship with Barbara had all the promise of delivering me from them and bringing me to a place where I would feel loved for the first time ever.

I didn't tell mother until after I was engaged, knowing that she would never approve. My mother was against everything

I did, except house cleaning and giving her most of my hard-earned wages, which at that time was more than eighty per cent of what I earned, including overtime. But now that I was engaged, that situation would have to change. I attempted to placate her by buying her a box of chocolates and trying to reason with her as to the rightness of my decision. She was unmoved, but I remained equally steadfast. As bad as our relationship was up to this point, (and it was bad) it was about to get much worse.

On a very cold and icy January day, just two months after our decision to get engaged, I went to Gerard Bradley, who ran the savings club in Weavex, and asked him if I could get my club payment earlier as I wanted to buy an engagement ring for my girlfriend. I felt so fantastic at the prospect of surprising Barbara with an engagement ring. The following Friday night we went to the pictures. I couldn't concentrate on the film because I was bursting to tell her the news that I was buying her engagement ring the next day. Suddenly, I blurted out, 'We're getting engaged tomorrow'. She never heard me and the moment was lost.

The following day, Saturday, we went to visit her sister Mary in Bluebell. I told her I had to go to the city on some important business and off I went to the jewellers in Henry Street. I found a beautiful and unusual ring, a set of six rubies with a diamond mounted above them. I just felt it was the perfect ring for her. The woman serving me was amazed that I even knew her finger size.

I returned to Bluebell with the ring, with no small degree of excitement, so much so that I was fit to burst. When I entered the house I asked Mary if I could have a minute with Barbara on my own as I had something special to give her. I

went into the sitting room where Barbara was sitting by the
fire. I knelt in front of her and handed her the ring box. She
opened the box, looked at the ring and said, 'Oh, that's lovely.
Who's it for?'

I was gobsmacked and deeply embarrassed at the same
time. 'It's for you,' I replied.

'Oh, that's nice,' she answered, and put the ring on her
finger. She then called Mary in to show her the ring. Mary
congratulated her and made us a cup of tea. I felt totally
deflated: it felt like an empty and meaningless experience
after such an emotional build-up. This was to be a sign of
things to come.

Over the next two-and-a-half years Barbara was to call it off
with me on numerous occasions. Each time, she would tell me
that she was testing me, while on other occasions she said I
was being too possessive. I *was* possessive, because I couldn't
handle the idea of her being with anyone but me. I never
realised just how terribly insecure I was and how desperate. I
don't beat myself up over it, because I know that I was
incompetent when it came to relationships. In fact, the
psychiatrist who would later carry out an assessment of me
described me as being 'socially inept' at the time. I must
admit to having felt aggrieved at this, but in actual fact he
was absolutely correct, and I think to myself, how could I
have been otherwise? It was as if I was more the girl and
Barbara more the boy when it came to expressing our feelings in this relationship — and the relationship was always
far more important to me than to Barbara, I felt.

Barbara and I went to see our local priest, Father Hughes,
in March 1979 with a view to getting married, but when I told
my mother, she said it would be over her dead body. She

resented the fact that I had chosen someone myself and was making my own decisions in life and, when we tried to discuss the matter with Father Hughes, he simply stonewalled us, telling us that he was not going to marry us. It transpired that my mother had been to see him, expressing her dissatisfaction at our plans: I was dumbfounded and very angry towards both of them for what they had done to us. I was nineteen at the time and it was to be another year and a half before we finally married.

Over the coming months, my relationship with my mother would deteriorate. I came in from work one evening and found nothing but hostility towards me because I had gone to see Father Michael Cleary to get some advice on how to deal with the situation. I mentioned to him my mother's opposition to my marrying Barbara, and he told me I was very mature and had given him excellent reasons for getting married. He promised he would talk to my mother and try and get her to see sense, but that is not how things transpired; at least not according to my mother. She told me that Father Cleary told her I was nothing but a troublemaker. I think she was lying. Either way, that really was the beginning of the end in terms of my relationship with her, if one could call it a relationship.

Things reached an all-time low when I was knocked down in a hit-and-run accident in October 1979. Barbara had called it off with me, again, for the umpteenth time. I was cycling up to work in a distraught state, crying much of the way. I was preparing to turn onto Airton Road when I was struck from behind. I knew nothing about it and was unconscious for quite some time. When I regained consciousness I found myself in a field surrounded by passengers from the number

77 bus. Apparently, the bus had been behind a van which had hit me and sped off. I was taken to hospital with some internal bleeding and cracked ribs, and was kept in for four days.

When my mother came in to see me, she had the most awful expression on her face. She never asked how I was. What she did say was that she was going to 'sort me out' when I got home. The reason? I had confided in my sister (a typically girlie thing to do) that I was having a physical relationship with Barbara. The situation between us became irretrievable after this. When I came home from hospital, I made it clear to her that I was not going to stay and suffer her injustice any longer, and I went upstairs to pack my clothes. She followed me, and, to my horror, she went for me with a knife telling me she would 'fucking kill' me. I knew then that I must leave the house. I packed all my belongings into a black plastic sack and was carrying it downstairs, but unfortunately, my mother intercepted me. She told me I wasn't leaving and followed me up to Barbara's house, all the way up Ballyfermot Road, telling me I was nothing but a 'fucking troublemaker' and that I would marry Barbara over her dead body.

When I knocked at the door, Barbara came out, but once she saw my mother standing outside the gate, she told me I should go home, that she didn't want any trouble. I felt like the ground had opened up and swallowed me, except that I now had to turn around and see the awful face of my mother looking smug and superior. What hurt more than anything, was the fact that I felt I could not depend on the very person I was marrying. My mother had been so enraged by my plans to leave that she had tried to stab me and my fiancée failed to support me.

The situation just went from bad to worse over the following months but, just as I had promised, I succeeded in leaving home, staying first with Barbara's sister Lily, before moving into the mobile home which I had bought with Barbara on the Killeen Road, with her parents' reluctant agreement.

One of the issues I discussed with Barbara was the number of children we would like to have. When she asked me how many children I wanted, I said that I would like five. Her reaction was to give me the most awful clatter across my face. 'I want at least twelve', she said. I replied that that was okay with me so long as we could afford to have that many. I thought we were all set for building a loving, happy and fulfilling family, despite the many problems we'd had along the way. There was definitely the prospect of having children and that made me immensely happy.

We finally got married on 27 March 1981. It was, to say the least, a lacklustre affair. Just two weeks before we were due to get married, my family announced that they were not coming to the wedding. My mother cried and said it was sad that they would not be there. I reminded her why they weren't coming — because of her attitude to my break for independence — and that this was never the way I wanted it to be. She relented and determined that she would be there, even proposing to have the reception in her house. For the sake of a possible reconciliation, I agreed.

On our wedding night, after a quiet meal at home, we left for our hotel. When we registered, I overheard someone saying, 'There's another Mr and Mrs Smith.' I was mortified. We headed for Killarney the next day, Saturday, to begin our honeymoon, which was remarkable for the almost complete lack of enthusiasm on Barbara's part; I knew that she didn't want to be there with me. I tried all manner of things to generate some interest in our honeymoon, but it was to no avail. I was completely clueless as to the real reason why. That was to come later. Now, I realise that we were both marrying for the wrong reasons. Barbara was desperate to get out of the house and away from her parents, and so was I — hardly a good foundation for marriage

However, the first few weeks of our married life were reasonably okay, though a little uncertain. But the next few months were to see a significant deterioration. It started with Barbara not wanting to do any kind of housework and on the occasions when she did, it was with the minimum of effort. It fell to me to do the cooking, cleaning, ironing etc. despite working long hours in Gilbey's. I had started working there after the Weavex factory had closed down and I was to stay there for the next twelve years.

The situation deteriorated to such a degree that I wasn't allowed near her without the use of condoms. This was a terrible blow, given the fact that she stated that she definitely wanted children.

Shortly after our honeymoon, we started saving for a house of our own, as we wanted to get out of the mobile home as soon as possible, but I was to get the most awful shock and one that was to reverberate through the remainder of my time with Barbara. It was a Saturday afternoon and I was resting in the sitting room of our mobile home. Barbara came in and started shouting at me: 'I hate you and I don't love you. I'm sorry I ever married you and I'm never going to have your children!' Words can barely describe the feeling of hurt and pure devastation which I felt. I later learned that Barbara's outburst was due to her realising that she had made a terrible mistake marrying me. She loved and cared for someone else and preferred to be with him. But she was not prepared to take responsibility for her mistake and tried on numerous occasions to pressure me into leaving, which I steadfastly refused to do. It was clear to me that she did not want to be seen as the one who had walked away.

It was impossible to focus on anything after that and at work I was reduced to tears thinking about what was happening at home, but was unable to explain why; after all, *men* are not supposed to tell their troubles to anyone. But, as difficult as the situation was, worse was to come and from a most unexpected source.

Chapter 7
The Violation of Purity

Do ye hear the children weeping, O my brothers,
Ere the sorrow comes with years?
They are leaning their young heads against their
mothers —
And that cannot stop their tears.
The young lambs are bleating in the meadows;
The young birds are chirping in the nest;
The young fawns are playing with the shadows;
The young flowers are blowing toward the west —
But the young, the young children, O my brothers,
They are weeping bitterly! —
They are weeping in the playtime of the others,
In the country of the free.
[ELIZABETH BARRETT BROWNING]

I was still struggling with the devastation caused by Barbara, when another devastating event unfolded. I had just turned twenty-one in June and received Barbara's bombshell a few weeks later in August, and then came one of the most awful events of my entire life. It was a balmy evening and I was coming home from work at around 10.30 p.m. after doing the evening shift. I was cycling towards the Church of the Assumption on Ballyfermot Road, when I saw my father standing outside with a suitcase. Of course, I went over to him and asked him what was up.

He said, 'That fucking mother of yours is causing trouble again. Can you give me a pound so I can get the bus into the barracks?' I knew better than to pry and left him off with a couple of pounds. My next stop was the house to find out what on earth was going on.

No sooner had I reached the sitting room when my brother James took me into the kitchen and told me that I was not to breathe a word to anyone of what he was about to tell me.

'Dad has been interfering with the girls.'

'What!? What do you mean he's been interfering with the girls?'

'He's been having sex with them…' Silence. What else could there be but silence. 'How many of the girls?'

'As far as we know, two.'

'Where's Mam?'

'She's down talking to Brenda and Martina and the other girls.'

Shocked, bewildered, devastated, appalled, sickened, dumbfounded. None of these can adequately describe the feelings that were running through me. The envy that I carried towards my sisters because of their closeness to my father paled into nothingness compared to the awful realisation of what they must have been feeling every time he placed them on his lap.

The more I thought about it, the more one of my sister's later actions began to make sense to me. She would come and sit on my knee from time to time and she would allow her hand to run down between my knees. I would be acutely embarrassed, but without ever realising where it was coming from. Now I realised its meaning and I was just distraught.

My mother came in and called us all together. She threatened every one of us with the direst consequences if we attempted to tell anyone about what had happened. And after the previous incident in which she attempted to stab me, I knew she meant what she said. She proceeded to intimidate us against telling even our own wives and husbands. My immediate thought was, how dare she do that to us? In the name of God, what were we supposed to do? According to her, it was none of our business and we were to stay out of it.

I could not believe that she could actually think that this devastating news would not have repercussions, which would go far beyond our house and would last for decades — for the rest of our lives. Whatever limited information we received then, our imaginations took over and ran riot. It was to be many years before my family were to face the full impact of what our father had done and the lengths our mother and my siblings went to in order to protect him; to protect this villain.

I went home in a complete daze and with my adrenalin pumping to the point where I thought my head and my heart would explode together. I tried not to say anything, but how could I not say anything? I went to bed. I kept tossing and turning and kicking the sheets as I often did when distressed over something or other. Try as I might I could not stop playing the images around in my head; images of what he was doing to my beautiful little sisters; my innocent little sisters. How dare he do that to them. Try as I might I could not stop the tears any longer, my breathing quickened and was shallower. I was hyperventilating. The tears came in floods and I kept crying: 'No, no, no, no, no, no, no, no!' Barbara kept asking me what was wrong. I tried not to tell her. But how could I not tell? Needless to say, I slept very little, if at all, that night and for many nights after. I realised that, ironically, had I been born the girl I so much wanted to be, I could have been subjected to the same abuse.

The revelations about my father's actions became an issue in our not having children, despite the fact that she had already made it perfectly clear that she never had any intention of having them. And she did this, knowing the deep hurt it was causing me. In fact, it got to the stage when it was hard to tell which of the two I cried for the most, that I felt so acutely the pain of my sisters' abuse, or the fact that I would never be a parent to my own children. This, with a strong sense of being trapped in a relationship, was proving to be more than I could bear and I felt I needed to do something drastic to enable me to cope.

It seemed to me at least, that we needed to deal with the revelation of my sisters' abuse as a family, and that we should all give them the fullest support and reassurance of our love. It is a shameful fact that this never happened and for years afterwards my sisters were to suffer alone, with the fear and guilt of hurting their mother if they dared to have their father charged, as he should have been. The only thing more disturbing than this was the lengths they and my mother went to to keep things quiet. The situation was so bad for my sisters that some of them were terrified to seek counselling for fear of how their mother would react.

It was obvious that my refusal to keep quiet about the abuse that had taken place meant I was no longer welcome in the family home and that my sisters wanted to avoid any mention of what had happened; despite the fact that they were still hurting because of it, this was easier for them to bear than the guilt of getting justice and hurting their mother in the process. It was after these revelations and my reaction to them that I believe I lost my sisters for ever.

Of course, secrets like these can only be hidden for so long, and ours was to come to light in spite of my mother's threats. The catalyst for this was an act of violence against one of my sisters' boyfriends, which resulted in the boyfriend and my sister, Sophie, going to the local Garda station to make a complaint. During the interview, Sophie was asked why she wasn't living at home, to which she broke down in tears and proceeded to disclose the sexual abuse she'd suffered at the hands of her father.

The first I knew of this was when she knocked on my door on a Sunday afternoon in a state of terror. She had obviously realised the enormity of what she had done and was in fear of her life. I promised her that I would stand fully behind her if she was telling me the truth, knowing full well that I was going to pay a high price for it, but she was my sister and there was no question of abandoning her at a time when she needed me the most. I went to the Garda station the next day and I made a statement, confirming what I knew up to that time, which was not very much, but it was enough to confirm what my sister had told them.

Word had gotten back to my parents that Sophie and her boyfriend were staying with me and Barbara, as they were terrified to go back to their flat. Another brother and sister came to my home and tried to speak to Sophie, but she was too terrified to talk to any of them. A few days after this she fled to Dingle with her boyfriend, thinking they would be safe. They were wrong and about five of my brothers and sisters went to Dingle to bring her back and to 'close off' the situation, as they saw it.

In the meantime, however, two garda detectives called to see me, looking for a fuller statement. I duly obliged, and then they told me they intended to go to my sisters' places of work in order to get statements from them. I was appalled and told them that that was completely unacceptable and that it would be too much of a traumatic experience for the two sisters involved. I proposed that I would accompany them and go into the supermarket where they both worked and have them both released by their supervisor.

The two detectives got fed up waiting and so came into the store. And before I got the chance to speak privately with my sisters, the two detectives were there and caused the very situation I'd been trying to avoid. I was left trying to explain the situation to two very upset girls who instantly blamed me for bringing the detectives down at my own instigation. It seemed that I was to be made a scapegoat for the family distress.

However, on the strength of my sister's brave revelation, a meeting was convened in my younger brother's house. I was excluded. During the meeting my brothers expressed the feelings I'd been encouraging them to express since the original disclosures had been made. And all, except one, openly admitted to being very badly affected. They revealed how they never saw their own children in the same way afterwards; how they were afraid to bathe them lest they, too, be accused of abusing them. In the meantime, the detectives went to my father with the statements made against him. I understand that he admitted to the allegations, but I believe that it was out of fear for my mother that my sisters relented from pressing charges against my father. That has remained the case until fairly recently when the case was reopened following the death of our mother.

This whole experience and my family's reaction to my desire to be open about it, served to reinforce the fact that I was not wanted as a member of this family. I was sickened by the way my mother went to such great lengths to protect my father at the expense of her children. From this point on I was resolved not to refer to her as 'my mother' and, indeed, that is how it ended between us.

Chapter 8
Living Apart, Together

Marriage is like life in this — that it is a field of battle, And not a bed of roses
VIRGINIBUS PUERISQUE [ROBERT LOUIS STEVENSON]

When I look back on those days and the events that were to unfold, I feel like such a complete idiot. I mean really, how many times does a woman have to tell a man that she doesn't love him before he gets the message? People who are desperate for love will do desperate things to be loved, even tolerating the most terrible behaviour and cruelty. In this respect I was very much the weak one in the relationship, but given my history and my sense of worthlessness and unworthiness, what else could I do?

I stayed in my hopeless marriage because I was convinced, on the one hand, that I could do enough to get Barbara to want to stay married to me; on the other, it was the absolute fear that if I left this hopeless relationship, I would be held responsible for something that was really not my fault. But there was also the plain and simple truth that I loved Barbara very much and simply could not countenance life without her, despite the overwhelming evidence that she never really loved me. Later on, my loyalty would be complicated by my being a committed evangelical Christian and all that that entailed in terms of the duty of a husband to his wife. But even that could not resurrect a marriage that had never really been a marriage to begin with.

Nonetheless, in the early 80s, we struggled on. We started to look at a few houses in January through April 1982 and finally settled on a house in Tallaght at 24 Homelawn Gardens. We decided to make an offer for it. It was £19,500 and we could just afford the deposit. Barbara was so intent on getting the house that she promised to start a family once we got out of the mobile home. This, of course, was all the motivation I needed to expedite the sale as soon as possible, which I did and we were ready to move in July of that year. I genuinely thought that our marriage was going to work and that Barbara would keep her promise to start a family. I was totally elated at the prospect of being a dad and would imagine what it would be like giving my love to my little son or daughter. I really didn't care which I had. What was most important was to be a father (as I thought at the time) and to help my children to become whole, rounded human beings who would make a positive contribution to the lives of those with whom they came into contact. It was important to me that my children's upbringing would be the total opposite to the way my parents had raised me, or rather, how I would have turned out had I not consciously withstood their years of abuse and bad example.

We moved into the house on a Saturday and our next-door neighbour came out to greet us, giving us some salt to throw over our shoulders on account of the superstition that it was bad luck to move into a house on a Saturday. I don't know about the superstition, but it is certainly true that the time we spent there was an unmitigated disaster. It was there that Barbara was to leave me for the first time and it was there that I was to have some of the worst experiences of our time together.

I never needed to be told that it was wrong to hit a woman. Violence of any kind was already abhorrent to me and I felt it should be used only under the most extreme circumstances, to the point that I would allow people to beat me stupid rather than hit them; I would not hesitate to use violence to protect those I loved, just like I did in defence of my younger brothers and sisters, but rarely for myself.

This attitude predisposed me to take a lot of verbal abuse and psychological pressure from Barbara without ever retaliating, except that is, to express my hurt and frustration at the way she would treat me. I succeeded in not retaliating, but this just made her worse. She used the death of her mother and missing Ballyfermot as her excuses.

Eventually, Barbara decided to return to Ballyfermot, to her parents' house, for a break. It was while Barbara was back in Ballyfermot that I experienced a strong need to dress as a female and of being unable to cope as a man. This had been a long time in coming and when it did, it never left me. On the contrary, it was to become more pronounced as the months and years wore on, despite my very best efforts to suppress it. It was during this period that I found myself unable to deny that there was a different *self* longing for expression; a deeply vulnerable, gentle, tender and sensitive self that needed above all to feel loved and wanted. But there was nothing or no-one to help me feel this way. The loneliness was sweeping over me in waves and my health was suffering because of it. I resented having to be strong all the time.

Barbara came back, telling me that she was only doing so because her father had told her that she had made her bed and had to lie in it.

During our time in Tallaght, I threw myself more fully into my studies with the Jehovah's Witnesses, in search of spiritual truth. Not the right place to go for it, as it transpired, so it was also in Tallaght that I became a born-again Christian and would remain one in one form or another for the next twenty or more years.

Looking back, I can think of several reasons why I became so intensely involved in religion at this time. One reason was that I could use it as a mask to hide my true *self*. I thought that I could use religion to explain why I felt the way I did. By accepting my gender conflict as part of my 'sinful' nature, I could repent of it and, through much prayer and fasting and confessing it to my pastor and some of my brethren, I could finally rid myself of it and get on with living a normal Christian life. Again, I was wrong, and continued to repress my true gender identity from myself and, I thought, from everyone else. It never occurred to me just how many people were already questioning this, but never letting on to me that they were. It was to be many years before I finally realised that my condition had absolutely nothing to do with me being a 'sinner', and the mental and emotional burden I had placed on myself became increasingly intolerable and certainly contributed to my later breakdown.

It was in April 1983 that I became a professing Christian, around the same time as Barbara's mother died. She was just 57 and died from emphysema. Barbara never really got over the grief of her loss and she completely shut me out and would not allow me to provide her with any comfort or support. Her father died three years later and again she was plunged into grief and again she shut me out. There was nothing I could do for her.

In 1987 things looked up briefly when Barbara found out that a local woman, Mrs Daly's, house on Ballyfermot Road had come up for sale. I never saw her so enthusiastic about my buying a shirt before! I had decided that I needed to dress up to go and see Mrs Daly about accepting our offer to buy her house, and bought the most expensive shirt I could find. Barbara assured me that if I succeeded in getting the Daly house for us, then she would definitely try for children. I was desperate to have children and so agreed to do everything in my power to get the house. I asked Mrs Daly if she would be willing to rent the house to us to give us the chance to save for a deposit. She agreed, and we managed to save for the deposit and buy the house outright less than a year later. I learned some years later that Mrs Daly thought of me very highly and always appreciated the way I continued to visit her long after we had bought the house.

I now turned my attention to starting a family and asked Barbara if she was going to keep her promise. I felt under pressure to buy the house in order to have the possibility of having children, something I had always wanted. But for the third time in six years, I was to be disappointed. The devastation I felt was only matched by the realisation that I was never going to be a parent while I was married to her and the fact that I was not prepared to leave her because of my faith meant that there was virtually no hope of me ever having children. I had to carry this loss in silence and amidst continuous queries about when I was going to start a family. To compound my misery I was frequently jeered in work by some of my workmates because I still had no children after eight years of marriage. They asked if I wanted them to come up and show me how to make Barbara pregnant. Words fail me to express how this made me feel.

It was 1988 when I noticed that Barbara and a neighbour were spending more time together. At first I didn't think much of it, but then I noticed that when we went round to our neighbours she started to ignore me. On one particular occasion, she started to mess with this neighbour. It was a hot day, and he got hold of the water hose and started to spray her with it and she never batted an eyelid, on the contrary, her enjoyment of it was all too evident. I was seething with jealousy and did nothing to hide it. I told her that it was inappropriate for her to be going around with a wet blouse. She told me to mind my own business.

A few weeks later we had a row over the way she flirted with the neighbour and I told her that I was not prepared to tolerate it. She responded by giving me a slap across my face. To my immense regret, I snapped and thumped her on the shoulder. A couple of days later, she left me and moved in with the neighbour. She stayed there for about three or four weeks. I called to see her one evening to see if I could talk her into coming home, but when I got there I saw her wearing the clothes I'd bought her for Christmas, but which, until now, she'd steadfastly refused to wear. Now she was wearing them while sitting alongside the neighbour, on the floor. Again, I pleaded with her to come back. She made her disdain obvious and told me that she did not love me and wanted me to leave her alone.

I returned home where my brother Graham had been waiting. I told him what had happened and, as I recounted the events, I came to the realisation that I could not allow her to continue treating me like a piece of shit under her shoe. I resolved to get myself together and move on; regrettably, my determination was short-lived. Barbara returned home but made it abundantly clear that she was coming back for the

house as she had no intention of giving it up and that I could
leave if I wanted to. That was never going to happen given
that I was a very committed Christian, something that was of
little help during this whole period. If anything, it made it
much worse: if I hadn't been a Christian, I might have been
able to end my unhappy marriage much earlier.

The only time Barbara and I ever really got on was after we
attempted to live separately in the same house, which we did
from 1984 until our separation in 1995. We came together
physically no more than three or four times a year. This, however, did not stop me from initiating counselling in the hope
that the marriage would work. I asked several pastors over
the years to counsel us with a view to saving our marriage. In
every single instance Barbara stated that she had made a
mistake marrying me and that she regretted the hurt it had
caused me. She told them that she was verbally abusing me
because she resented my persistent efforts to make the
marriage work when she didn't want to. The problem for me
was that I fully accepted this in my head but not in my heart.
I could not cope with being rejected by someone to whom I
had given so much of myself. It was wrong for me to keep this
up, but keep it up I did, though only intermittently. From
around 1990 onwards, Barbara encouraged me to find someone else to love. I knew that my marriage could not be saved,
but it would take time and more difficulties before I could
finally resign myself to that fact.

It was somewhat ironic that, years later, my mother would
confess to me that she felt guilty about the way she had
pushed me towards Barbara by being so resistant to us being
together. She also confessed that, had she brought me up to
think more of myself, to have greater self-worth, that maybe
I would not have tolerated Barbara's conduct for so long. She

stopped short of admitting that her own and my father's rearing of me contributed to how I allowed myself to be treated by others. It was absolutely true, but neither of them was prepared to admit to this; though that was to change some years later.

Looking back at the numerous times I encouraged Barbara to come shopping with me and the vast amounts I spent on buying clothes for her, I realise that I was really buying the kinds of clothes I would wear had I been able to do so. I loved shopping and especially looking at the latest fashions. I also loved the new choices of ladies' lingerie and how it was becoming much more feminine. I would use my purchases for Barbara as a cover for buying my own bits and pieces, mainly skirts and blouses, along with some lingerie. The sense of achievement and satisfaction I got from buying my own clothes bordered on the ecstatic. But that was short-lived as I felt increasingly guilty about it and would pray and fast, asking God to remove the urge to dress as a woman. I was convinced that He would, and there were times when it appeared to be working, as I would get these mad bursts of conviction when I would throw my lovely clothes into the rubbish bin. Unfortunately, it didn't work and the need to be Sara would come back, only more intensely than before. I threw myself deeper into my religious activities, especially praying and fasting and, the more I did this and failed to get the deliverance I so desperately wanted, the more preoccupied I became with it.

Chapter 9
Time to Grow

The spirit of self-help is the root of all genuine growth in the individual
SELF-HELP [SAMUAL SMILES]

It is amazing how we can develop and grow and never see it happen until we look back from where we came. That is what it was like for me in my twelve years working in Gilbey's. The things I would learn there, and the opportunities I got to develop as a professional, gave me some comfort at a time when my identity was in crisis. Although much of my time there was boring and unpleasant, there were quite a few reasons to look back and to be grateful.

My first job there was as a general operative, or, roughly translated, a general dogsbody. I worked on the back of 'A' and 'B' production lines, loading bottles and cases onto the lines. I also had to sit in the crow's nest, opening the flaps on the cases to allow them go through the packer, which dropped bottles into the cases and then sealed them before they moved along the conveyor belt to the palletiser in the warehouse. Another job involved feeding the Sig packing machines with flat boards, which were then made into cases for the bottles coming from the Jones machine.

We changed jobs every hour, but every one of those jobs was the most boring imaginable. I mean, how many cases can you load, how many pallets push and pull, how many boards can you feed into the magazines without getting stupid? My promotion to the position of relief operator was not much better. Watching thousands of bottles of Baileys Irish Cream going by day by day, week by week and year by year was not my idea of an interesting and purposeful occupation.

The longer I stayed at it, the worse I felt, to the point where I developed serious anxiety attacks every morning before going to work. Some were so bad that I curled up into the foetal position and stayed in bed. I could not face the point-lessness of the work I did and craved something that would be interesting and challenging.

After several years as a relief operator, I'd had enough and went back to being a general operative, mostly for the exercise. To overcome the boredom and to stimulate my mind, I began reading. The more I read, the more I wanted to read. I also looked for opportunities within the company that would get me away from the machines, so I volunteered to train as a first-aider and as a safety representative for the bottling-hall staff. I was sent away on courses and this became a catalyst to go on and do more courses and to look for opportunities to use my newly acquired knowledge and skills. Things were definitely looking up. I also sought out every opportunity to chat with my female work colleagues, which would be the high point of my day.

It was shortly after I started in Gilbey's that I became inter-ested in the Jehovah's Witnesses. It was whilst I was with them, that I acquired the discipline to sit and read with a purpose other than just learning to show I was 'normal'. I was passionate in my interest in learning and growing. Indeed, it is fair to say that I was somewhat impatient during this period. Reading gave me a view of life and people that enabled me to show discernment when dealing with difficult circumstances and it gave me the vision and strength to be different, which was very unusual for someone of my age. It did mean becoming rather serious-minded but never morose. It was during these years that I would seek out places where I could sit over a cup of coffee and a good book and just while away the hours, filling my head with new knowledge and new ways of looking at not just my own life, but the lives of those who had gone before. I was in heaven then and though I rarely get the opportunity now, I treasure the memory.

It was while I was in Gilbey's that I faced one of my biggest fears and put myself through college. I graduated with a diploma in industrial relations. I was very interested in the subject and made it my business to attend all our union meetings. One particular meeting was to change the course of my life for ever.

The union had been negotiating a wage agreement with the company and held a meeting in which they were recommending acceptance of the deal. I was convinced that it was a really poor deal and that we would do better to reject it and go back to the negotiating table. I went to the meeting all prepared with my calculator and notes. I had it all worked out in my head as to what I was going to say, but when the time came for me to speak, I was like a blunderbuss. I got up and just rushed the whole thing and was a cause of great merriment. I felt hugely embarrassed and humiliated. I vowed not to attend another meeting. My message was lost because of my inability to speak slowly and calmly.

However, my prediction about the wage settlement became a reality, which confirmed to me that I was well capable of analysing complex issues and coming up with the right conclusions and recommendations, even if I found it difficult to articulate them verbally. I resolved to do something about it. It was a life-changing moment as it made me even more determined to educate myself and to learn to write and speak properly. At this stage I was a practising Christian, having left the Jehovah's Witnesses in 1983, and regularly attending church. Just like I had done with the Jehovah's Witnesses, I jumped in with both feet and gave it my all. While study and work gave me a sense of personal worth that I had never experienced before, religion was my panacea.

I joined Lifegate Bible Baptist Church and had great ambitions for going into the ministry and training to become a pastor. I made it my business to attend every meeting and learn as much of the Bible as possible. I truly loved the studying and learned to study in a systematic way. I also learned how invaluable the importance of context is and this has stood me in good stead in the years since.

One of the requirements for preparing to enter the ministry was to have as broad an education as possible in matters theological and so it was that I built up an extensive library of all things theological and biblical, about church history and counselling, amongst others. In the Baptist Church, I felt that I had truly found a place where I belonged, where I fit in. There were many opportunities to teach and preach and I did so with great relish. I became a Sunday-school teacher and street preacher and door-to-door evangelist. It meant being out of the house quite a bit, which, under the circumstances, suited me very well. It did have its downside, though, in that I received a lot of slagging and ridicule but, such was the strength of my beliefs, that I was well able to cope with it all. In fact, it hardly cost me a second thought. Barbara was not anywhere near as interested in religious or spiritual matters

At Dublin Zoo, 1964. I'm the one on the left.

From the left, my nan, me, Peter, Fred, Damien, Brenda and our mother.

Taken after my uncle and aunt's wedding at the Church of the Assumption, Ballyfermot, c. 1971

Signing the Marriage Register at St Matthew's Church, Ballyfermot, 27 March 1981.

The Green Fields Hotel, Playa Del Inglés, Gran Canaria, 1999.

Taking the helm, Sousse, Tunisia, 2003.

After I had my first laser treatment to remove facial hair, 2005.

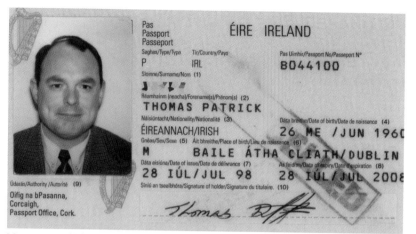

My passport, which would be altered after I changed my name by deed poll in September 2006.

Just one of the accreditations altered following my change of name by deed poll.

Taken at home in Midleton during a girlie night in, 2005.

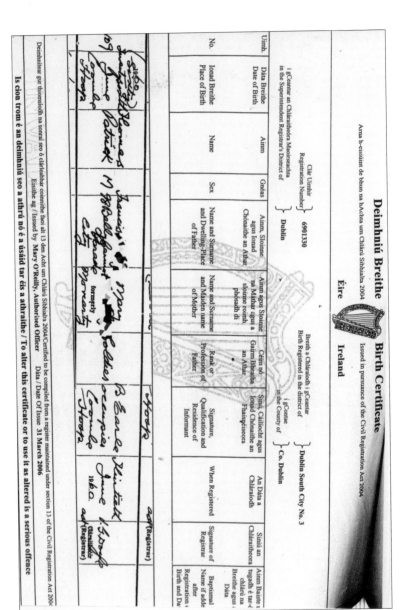

My birth certificate.

National College of Ireland

Diploma

in Industrial Relations and Trade Union Studies

Sara-Jane Cromwell

who completed this course under the direction and to the satisfaction of the
Lecturers of the College

Conferred this 12th day of September 1990

Joyce O'Connor

Professor Joyce O'Connor
PRESIDENT OF NCI

My new name on my first ever qualification.

I was invited to the National College of Ireland to have my Industrial Relations graduation photo retaken as Sara in October 2007.

Taken with RTÉ director Alan Robinson during the shooting of the 'Web of Desire' documentary, May 2007.

Taken with RTÉ presenter Anna Nolan, also during the shooting of the documentary.

My first time to vote in a general election as Sara, May 2007.

With my sister Clare, who met me for the first time as Sara in August 2007.

With my sister Sophie, who met me on the same day, August 2007.

At the photoshoot for the book cover of *Becoming Myself*, July 2007.

Happy being me.

and though she was encouraged by our pastor to come to church, she was indifferent for the most part.

It was while I was in Lifegate Baptist Church that Sara sought some experience of life once more. In fact, her need for expression became more urgent, now that I was seeking to enter the ministry. I have since learned that personal growth plays a part in the development of gender identity disorder in that, as your personality changes, your true gender identity becomes more pronounced. So, I started wearing women's clothes again and, despite my best efforts at resisting, I was unsuccessful in my attempts to overcome the need to dress.

This prompted me to confide in my pastor. His response was to tell me that we sin instinctively as children but that we get better at it as we get older. What this had to do with my problem I had no idea, other than to realise that he hadn't a clue how to deal with my situation. I was alone yet again in my efforts to understand and cope with my female gender identity. I not only had a wife who preferred other men to her husband, but I also had to cope with the guilt of being a sinner and the guilt of wearing women's clothes; something that is condemned in the Book of Deuteronomy. Of course, this prohibition does not apply to people with gender identity disorder, but I didn't know that at the time.

It was while I was a member of Lifegate that I met Peter Parkinson, pastor of Leeds Reformed Baptist Church. While I was in Leeds I was introduced to the work of the Caring for Life organisation, a Christian outreach group that provided homes for teenagers who had been turned out by the social services. Some were drug addicts, others were homeless and some were prostitutes. What they all had in common was their need to be given a home and a new chance at life, which no-one but Caring for Life was prepared to give them. It was through this organisation that I met a young fourteen-year-old girl named Mandy. Mandy was a prostitute and had HIV. She had been thrown out of her home by her mother for no other reason than that she was in the way. I felt that I could relate in some way to her vulnerability and difficulties, and all my preconceived ideas about the homeless, drug addicts and prostitutes were to be challenged through the time I spent with these young people. Being amongst them brought out my nurturing instincts and I volunteered to help out whenever I visited Leeds.

While I was busy developing myself spiritually, things were deteriorating in Gilbey's. It is fair to say that I'd set myself up for the many wind-ups I experienced during my time there. I was undoubtedly devout in my beliefs but I was also a royal pain in the arse in that every conversation was about religion; and if they weren't, then I manipulated them so they would be. I was all enthusiasm and no balance during those early years of being a Christian. But that was about to change and change dramatically.

The company was hugely successful in terms of making large profits and had experienced rapid expansion, but morale within the workforce was appallingly low. It seemed that, the more the company increased its profits, the meaner they were to their employees. People felt they counted for nothing and that there was nothing coming from the company that would enhance their work experience and motivation. There was little or nothing by way of acknowledgement of the workforce who had helped it to get to where it was. We had managers and supervisors who were becoming increasingly draconian, especially towards temporary workers, who were treated as second-class citizens by both management and other workers. I felt extremely angry about their treatment and vowed to do something about it. I decided to seek election as senior union representative to represent their interests. This, of course, meant doing something far more substantial than just preaching about what was wrong.

The shop stewards' committee, in my opinion, was not doing a good job. This led to a serious fall-off in attendance at union meetings. Morale was on the floor and there was nothing to be done, it seemed. It was during this period that I had been learning about Christian philanthropists and missionaries who brought the Gospel to the less fortunate in very practical ways and who brought about a great many changes and improvements in peoples' lives, including the abolition of slavery and so on. I also learned that there were quite a few religious people involved in setting up the various trade unions. I learnt that I could be spiritual *and* give a practical example of a living faith at one and the same time. 'By their fruits ye shall know them,' became a personal motto and made me determined to preach less and to practise more.

I had seen enough to know that all my predecessors had no formal training or qualifications for the position they held in trust. Rightly or wrongly, I held the view that it took more than good intentions and being Mr Popularity to represent those who would depend on me to act in their best interests. It was with all this in mind that I determined to return to college and get the diploma that I had not yet completed. It was a truly wonderful experience. I loved every blessed day of my time at the National College of Industrial Relations.

After I had received my diploma in October 1990, I determined to put myself forward for election to the position of senior union representative, but how was I to achieve this when so many union members showed a dislike of my preaching? This really was going to be an uphill battle, but I was determined. I decided to force the first election in over twenty years, which created a major stir, not just amongst the SIPTU membership but throughout the entire company. I managed to get over a third of the vote, which was absolutely amazing given how difficult it had always been until now to get any kind of genuine election and the fact that all those who voted for me were aware that I was a practising Christian. This gave me the encouragement I needed to stick with my goal. I was elected soon after as shop steward for the bottling-hall members. I was on my way. I had determined that a year from this date I would be elected senior union representative and I started working on it the morning after the AGM. I wrote the following on a piece of paper and kept it in a safe place: '*On this date next year I will be senior union representative.*' And I was. The following year I was elected by a majority of six votes.

One of the things I am most proud of during my period in office was increasing my majority from just six votes to a unanimous desire for me to stay in office, including, amongst them, my arch rivals. I was taken aback by the level of respect I received from all areas of management. Their respect for me made it much easier to resolve industrial relations issues, with some of them seeking my advice before holding interviews with employees who had to be disciplined for one reason or another. At least here I was in a good place.

In order to make a significant difference as senior union representative, I determined that I would have to take a very unorthodox approach to how I fulfilled my role. I decided to think like a company director and line manager. I'd always had a hatred for confrontation and so sought to bring an approach that emphasised our mutual interests rather than the old divisive mentality that had caused so much confrontation and distrust in the past. By doing this I was in a better position to understand the company's thinking and how to negotiate effectively with them, but without compromising on my loyalty and commitment to the people I represented. I wanted to change the way in which both sides viewed each other. I never accepted that we were always right and they were always wrong.

One of my proudest achievements as senior union representatives was to give encouragement to the craft unions and the staff association to enter into discussions on my proposal to create an inter-union group that would combine all our resources and strengths in dealing with our common interests and issues. This was a complete break from the old divisions that had existed. We set the group up and it was a great success. I was nominated as the senior spokesperson of the group and this meant being the principal negotiator on behalf of the group. This created a very positive atmosphere in which people felt hopeful for the first time in many years. It was truly groundbreaking and I was proud to have been a part of it.

A very great personal frustration for me working in Gilbey's was being surrounded by so many feminine women and by my need for female friendship. Their sense of style drove me crazy and reinforced the growing conflict I was feeling on a daily basis. Fridays and special days were the worst. The girls would make great efforts to look well and they succeeded. The problem for me was that I was so envious of them being able to dress as they wanted and to be so comfortable in their femininity. It was stressful and it was extremely difficult not to make comparisons. My own body language was also starting to become more pronounced as were my efforts to befriend the girls, which I did with a degree of success, until they became curious about how I knew so much about women's problems and being able to give them such good advice, especially in relation to the way they allowed the men to treat them so rudely. In some cases this was misinterpreted as me fancying them, which wasn't true and even if it was, there was no way I ever did anything about it. I really did just want to have some real girl friends and to feel that I fit in with them; to feel normal.

This period sticks with me for other reasons; it was the period when reading and writing became a major part of my life as did going to the National Concert Hall to see the National Symphony Orchestra. I have such wonderful memories of Handel's 'Messiah' and listening to Beethoven's Pastoral Symphony. I went to the theatre to see plays and to various concerts in the Gaiety and Olympia. I tried to share all these interests with Barbara, but she wasn't that interested in them, which made them rather lonely at times. Years later I took my friend Kathy to the NCH for her birthday and it was so exhilarating to have someone I cared about really enjoy the experience and be as excited about it as I was.

Chapter 10
Everything Changes

Tempora mutantur, et nos mutamor in fillis
Times change, and we change with them
[HARRISON]

Graduating from the National College of Industrial Relations was such a great experience that it motivated me to go on and do other courses, this time through correspondence. I took two diploma courses with Kilroy's College, one in business communication skills and the other in business administration. Between my spiritual growth and my academic achievements and life experiences, I was becoming a more rounded person, but I still hadn't the confidence in my abilities that others evidently had; everything I did came from that same determination to prove I was just as normal as everyone else and an innate desire to make some kind of a positive difference.

In 1989 I started to attend Grosvenor Road Baptist Church in Rathmines. It is the most affluent Baptist Church in the south of Ireland and it showed. I got involved in 'the Thursday Club, set up for the local children, who would come in and play games and learn from the Bible. I enjoyed the work and had some good fun with the children. I stayed with Grosvenor Road for a year and then moved on to the Evangelical Church Fellowship which met at the Dublin

Christian Mission, across from the Four Courts. I was very well received by the pastor, Liam Joyce, and his wife Sheena. Liam immediately recognised my potential as a pastor, but there was something else he recognised in me that affected him in ways which he did not disclose but had a significant impact on our future relationship.

In order to get to know each other better we went for a walk around the Phoenix Park. We walked and talked for about four hours and I shared my life with Liam in a very open and honest way. What I did not do at this time was confide in him about my wearing women's clothes and the fact that I was experiencing a gender conflict and the fact that I was also struggling with my sexuality. I was twenty-nine at the time and it was to take another several years before I would share this with him. In the meantime, Liam assured me that I had a very special purpose for my life and that God was going to use me in ways I could not even begin to imagine. He wasn't wrong there. I told him of my previous aborted attempt at sixteen to write my life story and how my mother, once she uncovered my notes, had taken them away and destroyed them. Liam told me that I should write my story and have it published; in fact, he was unusually insistent upon my doing it. He told me that he saw me as a 'pathfinder' and that this would mean treading a very lonely path, but that I would come back and show others the way forward. I could not have imagined just how accurate that prediction was to prove. It is fair to say that I am profoundly indebted to Liam and Sheena, not just for their friendship, but also for their significant contribution to my personal growth and development.

In 1992, Gilbey's announced that they were downsizing the business and closing the Naas Road plant and moving the operation to Nangor Road, and so I would be made redundant. This announcement exactly coincided with my deciding to apply to Bible training college in Wales. These were truly exciting times. And, after some months of counselling, it seemed that Barbara was actually becoming interested in us having a marriage after all. She even went so far as to commit herself to coming to Wales with me. With the announcement by Gilbey's, it seemed as if God was placing His seal on my plans. I was on a spiritual and emotional high and was feeling extremely positive about the future.

This positivity was overshadowed by tests Barbara had had done in February, just after I'd left Gilbey's. She was being tested for possible Multiple Sclerosis. We were not too troubled about it at the time, which optimism had more to do with not knowing the seriousness of this bloody awful condition. I left Gilbey's on 7 February and was feeling very excited about our future prospects.

On 30 March we received the devastating news: 'Barbara, you are MS positive'. That is exactly how it was said and was followed with a phone number for the MS Society in Sandymount. The doctor made no attempt properly to explain the diagnosis, or, for that matter, to give any kind of prognosis. She said we could get counselling from the MS Society. And that was that. Needless to say, nothing was ever going to be the same again.

My protective nature kicked in immediately and I put plans in place for us to cope with the situation. It is fair to say that Barbara was entirely passive throughout this whole episode. I felt that it was imperative that she learn as much as possible about her condition and what she could do to cope with it. I made an appointment for us with the MS Society and attended within a couple of days. It was here we learned about the true nature of the condition and what we had to look forward to as our future. Again, Barbara remained passive, almost nonchalant, in her attitude. I got her to join the MS Society and I joined with her. I made it my business to learn everything I could about the condition and agreed to join a steering group for the purpose of creating a new branch of MS Ireland in west Dublin.

One of my first decisions on learning of Barbara's diagnosis was to withdraw my application to the evangelical college in Wales. At this stage, Barbara told me that she had changed her mind: she had had no intention of ever going and she had decided this before I had been accepted. I was devastated at this news and went into a depression. Not only were my hopes of going into the ministry destroyed, but now I was faced with looking after a woman who neither loved nor respected me. It was too much to take, but take it I had to, because I still loved her and was determined to do the right thing for her, and because I took my commitments as a Christian very seriously.

So it was that I threw myself into the work of setting up a new branch of the MS Society with my colleagues on the steering group. We were hugely successful in establishing a branch that was second to none. One of our favourite activities was the social evenings. We booked a function room in one of the local hotels and brought members out for the night. They were very enjoyable events and extremely popular. I made it my business to visit members of the branch in their homes to see how they were and how we could help them. I was in a privileged position as members would take me into their confidence and share many of their intimate problems with me; some of which were quite shocking and very sad. I can say in all truthfulness that it was my work with the MS Society that prepared me for my own diagnosis and transition.

However, at the time, the situation looked bleak. I had no job and was facing the future as a carer for someone who did not love me and did not want to be married to me, who had already had one affair and had tried to leave with an old boyfriend for England and clearly resented me for my constant efforts at trying to make the marriage work on some level. What in the name of Jesus was I doing putting myself through all that? Why could I not have more respect for myself and leave before it got any worse? The answer is, I genuinely believed that God wanted me there and that he would turn it all around. In faith, God would deliver me from all these feminine feelings and from the need to dress. He didn't. My faith was under severe strain and was to be tested to breaking point.

I found it near-impossible to find another job after leaving Gilbey's and I was determined not to go back to being an operator or doing manual work. I couldn't anyway on account of having developed fibromyalgia, a muscular condition which prevented me doing physical work. It was time to learn new skills and get new qualifications. I applied for innumerable jobs and got the same reply each time: 'We don't have a position suitable for someone with your qualifications and experience.' It was dismal. The redundancy money was running out fast and it was imperative that I find something soon as our debts were mounting and the dole money was seriously inadequate to help us cope. So it was that I signed up for a FÁS course in business management. The course was run in Finglas so it meant a lot of travelling, but it was worth it. I remember my tutor, Joe Chaney, with affection. Joe took a shine to me and once told me that he had a soft spot for me. He told me that I would never be a millionaire but that I would be very successful in whatever I did. It was really nice to have someone believe in me like that.

Unfortunately, though, the course was doing very little for my job prospects and I was knee-deep in debt. The low point of that whole period in terms of money problems has to be the day I went to the city to buy myself a much-needed pair of shoes. Nearly all my shoes were completely worn out, with holes in the few pairs I had. There was a closing-down sale in a shoe shop on the corner of Mary Street and Henry Street. I saw a pair of boots for just £10 and decided to buy them. I felt some relief at the thought that I'd been so prudent, but it only lasted as long as it took me to get out of the shop and into the street. I stood facing the shop and agonised about whether to return the boots and use the £10 to pay off a bill. I decided to keep the boots and live with the guilt.

I finally got a job, as an insurance salesman with Canada Life, and from 30 March 1992, when Barbara received her diagnosis of Multiple Sclerosis, to my departure in August 1995, I committed myself fully to looking after her and did everything in my power to fight for her rights. It meant looking after the cooking, cleaning, and collecting her Ensure energy drinks, her incontinence pads and so on. It also meant sitting around waiting to see politicians to get them to lobby for her benefits and to get her a home help who could assist her while I was at work. I also got her two dogs for company as she had been saying for years that she would love to have dogs around the house.

With all of this pressure, I came very close to my first ever serious mental breakdown, in April 1992. I was having an epic struggle with my cross-dressing, as I understood it then, and my faith seemed utterly useless to cure me of it. No matter how much I prayed, fasted, attended church, prayer meetings, conferences, preached, did street and door-to-door evangelism, Sunday-school teaching, had quiet times and so on, nothing could deliver me from this increasing need to be a woman. I was so desperate for God to deliver me from this gender conflict that I would prostrate myself on the floor of my study and, with outstretched arms, cry my eyes out to God, begging Him to deliver me from this great sin. I cried so much and spent so much time pleading and begging that I left myself an emotional wreck from it.

There were times when I would get a sense of euphoria at the belief that God had, in fact, heard me and that I had the strength to resist the temptation to dress and feel like a woman, and while I was in that state, I would take what few women's clothes I had and dump them. For a few days at least, I would have some peace, but it was a false peace as the conflict returned yet again and the need to buy and wear clothes returned, only stronger. My former pastor and Barbara were the only two people who knew about my continuing struggle with this issue and Barbara was completely indifferent to it.

In 1994, I was given a much-needed boost by being awarded the Trainee of the Year award by FÁS, for developing a system for helping people to work through their debt problems and writing a book on the subject of family finance, having completed an enterprise skills course at Ballyfermot Training Centre. I was allowed to bring two people to the awards ceremony so I asked Barbara and my regional manager at Canada Life. He told me he was honoured to be asked and I was thrilled he felt that way about it. But still I had my doubts. I was wrong.

On the day of the awards ceremony, we were escorted around the side of the presentation area, which was closed off with screens, but through a gap in the screens I could see the scrolls and plaques. It suddenly began to dawn on me that this was serious. When we reached the presentation area we were greeted by a lot of people, including some dignitaries and members of the press, along with photographers. I was called up to receive my scroll and plaque. I received a Trainee of the Year certificate and an award for excellence. I was beside myself with delight. I was then asked to pose for photographs and to give an interview to the papers, especially the *Ballyfermot People*, who highlighted the fact that, of the 1800 trainees that went through the various courses that year, only two from Ballyfermot were considered to have excelled. This really was a red-letter day for me and one I remember with great affection and appreciation.

It was ironic that great professional success happened at the same time as I was battling my personal demons, but it was in the summer of 1994 that I finally focused on getting help with my cross-dressing or at least to discover whether I was gay and if this could help explain my strong feminine instincts, which were growing stronger by the day. I heard of a nightclub at the Ormonde Hotel called the Temple of Sound and that there were men there who dressed as women. I went along to see what was happening and if I could answer some of the questions that had been vexing me for so many years. It was the first time I had ever kissed a man and it felt okay. But as the man was dressed as a woman, it still didn't answer the question about my sexual orientation. What it did do was help me to realise that I definitely was *not* a transvestite or cross-dresser and that my problem was something completely different. The difficulty now was that I really hadn't a clue where to go and get the help I needed.

However, other events were to take over and distract me. It was during 1994 and early 1995 that I made my last efforts to salvage something from my marriage, but to no avail. It was on Christmas Night 1994 that I accepted that the marriage was, in fact, dead, but it was to be a few months more before I finally gave up on it for ever.

It was nigh impossible to share with anyone what was happening in my life at this time. All my Christian friends were interested in doing was quoting passages from the Bible and reminding me of my duties to attend church and to take care of Barbara. Prayer was to be the answer to everything. But it wasn't for me. Everyone knew where I lived and how to contact me when they wanted my help with preparing CVs, job interviews, advice on Bible study and Sunday-school preparation etc, but not with providing me with the warmth and support I needed. I was desperate to go for a drink, or meet for a coffee, just to talk, to no avail. All of which made my sense of isolation and loneliness harder to bear, especially as living with Barbara was getting worse by the day and my health continued to deteriorate.

The loneliness was consuming me, in the way a black hole consumes everything that comes into its orbit. I was heading towards the abyss and the terror of it was, I could see it coming and there was nothing I could do to stop it. It seemed that there was no-one to help me, not my family, not my wife, not my church or my so-called friends. I simply couldn't communicate my distress to anyone.

I began to feel that the Christian message was irrelevant to the needs of people such as me, suffering all manner of trials and tribulations, unemployment, financial difficulties, family problems, health problems, crises of faith etc. What mattered more was that you had the right theology, the right church attendance; that you hung out with only the right brethren, that you went to the right sort of conferences and seminars, and that you remembered your place as a miserable, unworthy sinner. But Liam and Sheena Joyce and Chris and Helen Robinson were the exceptions to this rule. They showed us immense kindness and I am forever grateful to them for all their support.

But there was no support from either of our families. The exception was one of Barbara's sisters, who had many problems of her own. Yet she was the one who provided us with the most practical help and was by far the most generous and supportive. When she went shopping she would bring some food items for us as a gift. She would call in and spend several hours at a time keeping Barbara company and helping out around the house. The trouble with this help was that it wasn't always the kind of help I needed.

There was no emotional support, no friendship in the way I needed it. I needed to have a best friend and confidant, not just a counsellor. I needed friends with whom I could go for a meal, walk and talk about other things apart from the Bible. I needed people who would call me on the phone to see how I was and not just to talk religion. Nor did I need people constantly reminding me of my Christian duty to look after Barbara. Of course they were not to know about her behaviour or for that matter the affairs, nor the violence and verbal abuse. If I was to leave her, I would simply be that 'bastard' who left his disabled wife.

All the strenuous efforts I had made to try to make our relationship and marriage work were brought to a sudden halt on

Christmas night 1994. One of our neighbours had been invited in to have a Christmas drink with us. The evening was pleasant enough and there was not a sign of anything being amiss; nothing to arouse my suspicions. In fact, it was strangely nice to have Barbara being so civil to me. But all that changed around midnight when Barbara went to the kitchen with the dishes to do the washing up — an unusual event in itself — and the neighbour offered to help, as I had prepared the food. They were away for a considerable length of time and I was becoming increasingly concerned. I felt more and more that something wasn't right, so I went into the kitchen to see if everything was okay. As I walked towards the kitchen, I could hear them muttering and Barbara telling the neighbour that she really did fancy him. He told her he felt the same and then I heard the ruffle of clothes. My heart was pounding as it dawned on me that they were fondling each other. When I put my head round the door, they were kissing and had their arms around each other in a tight embrace. Her hands were fondling his bottom.

In an instant I knew that all my efforts at trying to salvage something from the situation were a complete waste of time. I confronted them while they were still cuddling each other. The neighbour was mortified about being caught and tried to let on that there was nothing between them, only making himself look absolutely pathetic in the process. Barbara, on the other hand, was quite brazen and made no attempt to disguise how she felt about him. The game was well and truly up for all of us and I really was in a complete emotional melt-down.

I felt a state of panic on the one hand and feelings of elation on the other. Here was the proof, if proof were needed, that she really did not love me or want me. It couldn't have been clearer. But what to do about it next was the problem. In the meantime, the neighbour stopped coming in and Barbara made her resentment obvious, blaming me because he would not come in to see her.

Over the coming days I had to come to terms with the whole ugly situation, and added to this was the fact that all my earnest prayers, fasting, loyalty and faithfulness were to prove utterly useless. Aristotle's words were to taunt me: 'good deeds shall not go unpunished'. From this point on, my life was to enter into what I call the 'winding-down' phase. By that I mean I developed a deepening depression and an overwhelming sense of despair, compounded by a growing crisis of faith. All my years of believing and serving the gospel, of church-going and witnessing, of prayer and fasting and the ridicule and rejection I faced constantly because of my public profession of faith, all came to naught. I really did have nowhere to go and no-one to go to for comfort and support. I was absolutely alone and desperate.

Part Two
Letting Go

Chapter 11
A Time to Leave

And who can tell but heaven, at last,
May answer all my thousand prayers,
And bid the future pay the past
With joy for anguish, smiles for tears?
FAREWELL [ANNE BRONTË]

I first got to know Maria through a phone chatline in early
1995. The conversation I had with her was to prove the
first life-changing event in a life-changing year.

No doubt there will be those who will smirk at the idea of
my using chatlines, but at this point it was either do that or
drink and drug myself into oblivion. It wasn't ideal and
under normal circumstances I would never have done it, but
these were far from normal circumstances. I felt so isolated,
so rejected, and so lonely, and the irony is that using a
chatline and getting to meet Maria most likely saved my life;
I am certain of it.

The more I shared with Maria about Barbara's illness and
its debilitating effects, the more she demonstrated her concern. When I had shared with her the very difficult financial
situ-ation that we were in, Maria vowed to help me. When I
confided in her that Barbara was drinking and smoking our
money away, Maria sent her £80 and one hundred cigarettes,
which Barbara accepted without showing even the slightest

appreciation. In fact, she had to be shamed into phoning Maria to say thank you.

It was in April of 1995 that I noticed a serious deterioration in my health. The panic attacks were getting much worse and my depression was deepening, to the point where I was no longer contemplating suicide as a thought, but was now considering how best to do it, when and where. The frequency of the panic attacks was increasing and with this came a very noticeable increase in pains in my head. On one occasion the pain was so bad that I was convinced I had a brain tumour. Once, I was driving from my office along the South Circular Road, towards the junction with Clanbrassil Street. The pain was truly overwhelming and my vision was blurring. It was very difficult to drive. I stopped the car in the middle of the road and got out, walking around for a few minutes while other cars had to drive around mine. I eventually got back into my car and drove home.

Barbara had a dinner ready for me but I could barely look at it, never mind eat it. 'What's the matter with you?' she asked, in her usual indifferent tone. I was unable to answer and my head collapsed onto the plate of hot food. I remained like this for a few moments and then made my way to bed. At this stage the pain was worsening and I was also feeling very sick in my stomach. As I lay on the bed I curled up into the foetal position and swayed back and forth.

Barbara eventually came into the room and sat in the chair by the window without saying a word. After a few minutes, she asked if I wanted a doctor, but I was unable to answer. She then said that I could suit myself and left the room. A few minutes later she came back in, at which time I was in floods of tears and convulsing. She looked at me and asked for money for dog food. She never called an ambulance. I could hardly believe my ears.

The next morning, I went to see my GP in order to get some help. He promised me that he would get me into counselling and prescribed Prozac. He never got me the help and I came off the Prozac very soon after, because I was having bad side effects. This meant trying to cope without any medical intervention whatsoever. It was indescribably difficult trying to function on a day-to-day basis. Work was also becoming more and more stressful and I was getting ever nearer to my breakdown.

Maria contacted me a couple of days after our conversation about my difficult situation and asked how we were getting on. I told her about what had happened over the past few days and she was shocked and concerned. So much so that she travelled all the way from Limerick to lend her support. It was then that she invited Barbara and I to go to her home in Newcastle West for a weekend, as she felt a change of scenery would do us both the world of good. She had no idea how bad our relationship was at the time and all she knew from me was that I was trying to be as loyal as I possibly could under very difficult circumstances. I hadn't let on about the events which had taken place at Christmas and their effects upon me.

We both accepted Maria's invitation, but as was so often the case, Barbara changed her mind and suggested that I should go on my own as I needed the break more than she did. I had mixed feelings about this, but I was happy at the prospect of getting away from Dublin and the whole situation.

Maria lived in a cottage which was just up the hill, off the main street in Newcastle West. It was very quaint and it was definitely designed for shorter people! I lost count of the number of times I banged my head going through the doorways and coming up and down the stairs. I loved the house and the back garden, where we spent some time talking and getting to know each other better.

As I got to know Maria better, I could not help liking her, but I also learned of how sad her own life was and how she had been through the mill herself. She had recently had an operation on her womb to remove cancer. The cancer eventually took her life some years later, at just 48 years of age. As I would later discover, Maria was also mentally ill, and this illness led her into actions that were not normal and caused a great deal of distress and hurt for other people. Maria suffered from multiple personalities and it was under this influence that she did many strange things. That said, there is absolutely no doubt in my mind and the minds of others who knew her that she genuinely did not know she was doing the things she did. Maria was also the first person who had been a real friend to me, and for that I am truly grateful.

While I was on this weekend break I felt a growing sense of the full enormity of how damaged I was and how my life had been one unbroken stream of abuse and rejection. My feeling was that they were the root cause of my complete lack of self-worth and confidence. It was this abuse and its effects, I thought, that made me feel useless and feel that I must always prove myself to everyone around me. For the first time since being a teenager at the holiday home Coolure House, I felt I could not cope with going back to Dublin and the people who had collectively destroyed me. I was dreading the return so much that I told Maria I could not cope with the thought of going back. She told me I didn't have to and so I phoned Barbara to say I was staying over an extra night. She was indifferent.

But ultimately, I knew that I had to return to Dublin and to reality and so I braced myself for the trip. Before heading back, Maria and her husband Doney said they hoped we would both come down for the holiday in August, but that even if Barbara opted not to come, I should still have my holiday. They felt that I really needed the break. They were right.

During my visit to Maria she told me about Reiki healing, a Japanese technique for reducing stress by the laying on of hands. She was a practitioner and offered to do a session with me. I accepted, although I was very apprehensive and sceptical. The next day Maria did a session with me in the parlour. It was a truly amazing experience and not at all what I expected. What shocked and intrigued me was Marie's ability to feel my pain and from that pain to identify some of my most secretly held experiences of personal suffering. It was an intensive experience but one that brought me tremendous release from pain. The benefit of the session lasted a couple of weeks, at which time the pain returned.

As I approached my birthday in June, Maria sent me a gift token of a meal for two in the Green Isle Hotel. Of course, I asked Barbara to come with me. She looked the best she had for a very long time and the evening was genuinely pleasant, no doubt helped by the fact that I had now accepted that we no longer had a marriage and never would have; that we were to be nothing more than friends thereafter. But inside, I was burning with the pain of rejection and was at a complete loss as to what to do next. I had to come to terms with the reality that I was never going to experience any meaningful love from Barbara and that she had, in fact, made a momentous mistake in marrying me. I also had to face the equally diffi-cult truth that I had married her for the wrong reasons. I was so terribly desperate to get away from my mother and father that I would have done anything and loved anyone in order to escape. This was wrong, just so, so wrong in every way.

And yet, even though Barbara and I were no longer 'married' in the true sense, I persisted in putting on a front, especially for the church. This, too, was wrong, but I was at a loss as to what to do. I was a practising Christian and I had a duty to God to be a good witness in every aspect of my life. I was prepared to do my duty as a Christian, no matter how high the price. This meant carrying the cross of suffering which was my false marriage.

It was also in June, a Wednesday afternoon to be exact, that I came home from work early because I had been feeling very low and unable to concentrate. I arrived home to find Barbara sitting in her rocking chair. I went over and stood by the window and asked her how she had been that day. She said that she was feeling fine and asked how I was. I told her that I felt very strongly that I was reaching the end of the road, that I simply could not go on for much longer and that I truly felt I was dying inside, that it was only a matter of time before I ended my life. Her response still affects me to this day. She simply rocked back and forth in her chair and said: 'Well, you know I don't love you, don't you?' There really was nothing more to say after that. The only two things I had to look forward to on the horizon were entering into member-ship at Grosvenor Road Baptist Church and my long-awaited holiday in Limerick.

By the time I got to Limerick, following my difficulties back in Dublin, I have to admit to being far nearer to the edge of reason than I had first thought. It really didn't take any-thing much finally to push me over the edge. I never saw it coming, but when it did, it was truly horrific.

It was a Thursday morning and Maria was out of sorts. For some strange reason she started going on at me about my family and railed at me because I wasn't getting on with my parents. I was completely shocked by this, not realising that that was to be the straw that would break the camel's back and become the catalyst for what followed.

She left the house to go up to town on some errands. I was alone and was thinking about what had happened earlier. The more I thought about it, the more foolish I felt at having taken her into my confidence about my childhood and what had transpired. The more I did this, the more stupid I felt and began calling myself names. The rush of memories and feelings that overwhelmed me was like a tsunami. I was caught in a barrage of voices shouting and screaming at me: *You stupid fucker! You stupid idiot! You useless bastard! You fucking spa head! You're nothing but a fucking troublemaker! When will you ever learn, you bleedin' retard?* All of these voices, were screaming at me while I punched myself all over my face. And the louder the voices the more vicious the punches became. The blackness came ever nearer with every verbal and physical assault. I was now pummelling my face and shouting the vilest names at myself; except that it wasn't me calling myself these names. It was them; my mother and father, my brothers and sisters, my so-called friends, the teachers, the nuns, the Christian brothers, my so-called work-mates. It was all of them together.

As I punched my face with both fists I shouted all manner of obscenities at myself:

'You stupid fucking bastard!'

'You fucking retard!'

'You are nothing but a spa head!'

'You're stupid!'

'You're an antichrist!'

'You're nothing but a fucking nuisance!'

'You're nothing but a mistake and you shouldn't be here!'

And so I went on, abusing myself verbally and physically and it was awful; so awful, in fact, that my mind started to go; literally. I entered into a phase where I was blacking out mentally. It was as if I was entering a mental black hole; oblivion. The best thing I could do was enter the hole, not that I had a choice, as it began to engulf me, and as it did, I allowed myself to be drawn into it. And as I was drawn into this black void, my mind began to lose its consciousness. I was entering the mental abyss and there was nothing to stop me.

That is, until Maria came home and heard my screaming from downstairs and rushed up to see what was wrong. The sight must have been terrifying for her and, in fact, she froze for about five minutes without knowing how to deal with the situation. Here was this man of six feet, standing on his bed, beating himself to a pulp and in terrible convulsions and this woman of just four feet something not knowing what to do, except to reach out her hand and call out to me.

I barely remember her touching my hand and ever so gently getting me to step down from the bed and sit down. She called my name over and over: 'Tom, Tom, Tom. What is the matter? What's wrong with you, Tom? What's happened? Tell me what's happened!' But I couldn't. I was unable to answer. Her voice seemed to be coming from a distance and I was unable to respond. I really don't know how long this went on for, but I do remember her getting me to say my name over and over again. 'What is your name? Thomas, tell me your name. Please say your name.'

More time passed and as it did so I gushed floods of tears as my body began to shake violently. But Maria kept calling me and, as she did, she held my hands more tightly and refused to let me go. It was as if she, too, could see the engulfing darkness and was determined to stop me from being swallowed up. Had she failed then, that would have been the end of me.

The darkness receded and her voice became clearer, and, as it did, I began to respond by saying my name. Slowly but surely, the convulsions stopped and I was left with the tears flowing freely down my face. Maria got me some tissues and began stroking my hair in order to soothe and comfort me, something I had not experienced in all my life. I was in an emotional twilight zone. She got me into bed and left me to rest, coming in at regular intervals to check on me. I can't remember anything else until I woke up the next morning. Maria insisted that I stay in bed and rest while she brought me up some food, but I was barely able to eat it.

Later that day Maria came to my room and told me she had arranged for me to go on a three-day break to Lahinch, after which I was to be taken to a psychiatrist for a consultation. The consultant was based at Barrington's private clinic in Limerick city. I was completely gobsmacked at this level of generosity. It was quite beyond me and I simply did not know how to cope with it or how to respond.

We arrived in Lahinch on the second Tuesday after my arrival to Newcastle West.

On our first night in the hotel, Maria was on the phone speaking to someone — it turned out to be my mother. Concerned for my welfare, Maria had made the decision to contact her. I told Maria that I did not wish to speak to her, but Maria insisted and so with great reluctance I did.

What my mother really wanted to know was why I was going to see a counsellor and what I was going to discuss with him. I told her it was absolutely none of her business and that I did not wish to speak to her any longer. She then threatened me that something would happen if I dared to reveal anything about what my father had done to me or to my sisters. I was trembling and could not wait to hang up the phone, which I did with great relief.

I received another call about ten minutes later; this time from my brother, Fred, who to put it mildly, expressed his deep displeasure. I hung up the phone and tore into Maria for making contact with them without my prior knowledge or approval. Only after doing so, did she realise how terrible my family were to me. She was shocked and could not comprehend how they could be so completely unloving towards me. It made no sense to her. But the damage was well and truly done by now and I was terrified of what would happen next. I reached a point where I felt I must do the only thing that was left open to me if I was ever to have peace. I decided to end it all there and then.

I told Maria that I was going for a walk, that I needed to be alone. I left the hotel and walked down to the beach. It was midnight and there was no-one around. I went straight into the sea and walked until the water was up to my waist. I just stood there thinking about what I really wanted to do, but also thinking of Maria in the hotel on her own and what would happen to her if I let myself drown. I felt it wrong to do that to her and so returned to the hotel.

When Maria saw me, she freaked out. She screamed at me that she was terrified of anything happening to me. Somehow, we got through the next three days and returned to Limerick. I was then taken to see the consultant in Barrington's. He asked me how I had come to be in Limerick and so I told him the whole sorry story. About the years of abuse, the abuse of my sisters and how that was affecting me. I told him about the phone calls and the threats and about my breakdown a few days earlier. I also told him of my 'cross-dressing' — as I thought it to be at the time. He could not have been blunter with me: 'If you stay in Dublin, you will die. I cannot treat you from there so you will have to decide if you want me to treat you. If you do, then you will have to decide to move to Limerick.' I told him I was prepared to do whatever it took to get the help I needed. He then told me that the hardest decision I had to make was whether or not to leave, and harder still would be carrying out that decision. He certainly wasn't wrong about that.

I returned to Dublin on the following Saturday, determined to sort out my situation once and for all. Barbara was pleasant enough and she said she had missed my company. I was careful not to misinterpret her meaning. I told her about all that had transpired and she responded with her usual indifference. I then proceeded to tell her of my decision to leave Dublin in order to receive treatment from the consultant and of his advice to me about leaving. She told me that it was the right thing for me to do. She then said that she would miss me, which I found surprising. The next day I put my plans into motion and began sorting out my affairs

On the Friday before I was due to leave, I called into Tesco to say goodbye to one of my sisters, Rachel. I told her that I could not tell her all the reasons for my leaving but that I would miss her. We had once been close, and I used to sit on the bed and listen to her as she confided her boyfriend troubles to me. Now, she was very hostile and tried to ignore me. It was a very difficult moment and I left knowing that I might never see her again and that the situation between us would never be resolved. But at least it wasn't for the want of trying on my part.

Friday arrived and I began packing my car with my clothes, computer and a few books and some other bits and pieces. The few days prior to this were completely awful: as bad as the situation was between us, I really did feel sorry for Barbara and felt the pain of our final separation, to the point that I was traumatised as I drove down the long road to Limerick. What made it worse was the fact that she never actually believed that I would do it. She tried to wish me well but I could see that even she was in a distressed state, which merely made me feel even worse. I had to remind myself of all that she had done and of the affairs, the leaving me for other men, the endless arguments and her indifference to my sufferings and feelings. And then there was Charlie and Dino, our two dogs. It tore at me so much to have to say goodbye to them. There is no denying that they knew something was wrong and they kept a very close eye on me.

As I left the house, I gave Barbara a hug and wished her well. I was determined that there was going to be no acrimony on my side at least. I thought there was to be none on her side, but was to be woefully disappointed later on. As I was leaving, she began to cry, but it was far too late for tears.

Chapter 12

A New Beginning?
Maybe

Voilà le commencement de la fin
This is the beginning of the end
[CHARLES-MAURICE DE TALLEYRAND]

I had a breakdown. I didn't ask for it, plan it, welcome it, or enjoy it — who would?— but I did have a mental breakdown and it very nearly cost me my life. There now, I've said it and the world did not come to an end, my true friends have not deserted me, and I am not alone in the world. But it really could have been so awfully different. It seems incredible but in so many ways I'm grateful for that breakdown, simply because it saved my life at that crucial period. It made me wake up and do something about my situation with Barbara and with my family. It had little to do with my gender identity at that time as I was still repressing that part of my *self.* But there is no doubting that the breakdown and all that subsequently emanated from it started me on a journey that has brought me to where I am now. It is so sublimely wonderful to be where I am today because of nature's intervention, and, as I'm now learning, the spirits who have been looking after and protecting me all this time. I should be dead so many times over, but I'm not; in fact I could not be more alive!

I drove away in my brown Mini Metro that day, with feelings of deep distress giving way to elation then back again. It was truly awful. I really had no idea what I was letting myself in for, but I also knew that I had reached the point of no return. And so I left Dublin for good. Now I had to work on the effects of thirty-five years of continual abuse, vilification, slander, physical violence, threats and constant rejection. This whole situation was compounded by the fact that I was suppressing my female identity, albeit with great difficulty. The overwhelming issue for me now was survival. As much as I felt my true identity was being ignored, I would simply have to fight to stay alive, every hour of every day for well over a year. And for quite some time to come, circumstances would intervene to make it impossible for me to go to that place within myself, to be the woman I was meant to be.

I seriously considered driving the car into a wall or a ditch and ending it all, but something kept me going to journey's end. It was Friday 31 August 1995.

When I arrived at Maria's house, she showed me to my room and prepared a meal for me. While I was unpacking my clothes I kept breaking down emotionally and felt completely overwhelmed by the enormity of my situation. I found it impossible to believe it was ever going to get any better. And for a while, I was right. The whole situation was just too much to cope with and so I resolved to put an end to it for once and for all. There was no question of me ending my life violently; that was for men to do, not me. There would be no hanging, shooting or driving my car into a wall or off a pier. On the contrary, it would be done gently and with dignity, there was to be no mess, just a quiet departure. I thought of how much better off everyone else would be when I was gone. I had absolutely no doubt that my family would have been relieved by my departure from this life. Their consciences would be silenced with my silence. I went to bed around seven o'clock. I took my Rivitril tablets, which I had been prescribed for panic attacks, and nearly all of my supply of Aspirin with some alcohol. Slowly but surely, I became unconscious and my body became cold and turned blue.

It was at this stage that Maria had come to my room to check on me and to see if I had settled in. she knew immediately that something was seriously wrong. She could see that I was unconscious and that my body was changing colour. She saw the empty tablet bottles and knew that I had overdosed on my medication. I can only imagine what went through her mind on discovering me in this condition, but she felt strongly that there was not enough time to get an ambulance, and get me to hospital, so she and her husband Doney took very drastic action to bring me round.

In order to revive me, Maria and Doney dragged me from my bed and took me downstairs. They put me into a very, very cold bath in order to shock me back into consciousness. I started to come in and out of consciousness and as I did Maria poured cider vinegar down my throat. This was to get me to vomit up any tablets that may have been in my stomach. I vomited for quite some time and eventually was taken back to my bed. Maria sat and watched over me that whole night and used a hairdryer to keep my body temperature right. It worked and I managed to sleep safely and soundly for the rest of the night.

Some people will say that Maria took very serious and dangerous risks in handling the situation as she did, and some might argue that she could have cost me my life. But I am convinced that she did exactly what needed to be done in order to not only save my life but also to prevent me from having to enter a psychiatric ward, which would most certainly have been a blight upon my life to this day. It wasn't for me and Maria saved me from it. For that I am eternally grateful.

As extraordinary as it seems, Maria made sure that I was able to get up the next morning, to start a new job which I had secured in the Coach House. She felt that it was essential for me to get on with living a normal life and making sure I could earn a living. Was I thankful to her for all she had done? No, I have to say that I wasn't in the least thankful. On the contrary, I resented having to cope with getting to work as I felt anything but fit for it: all I wanted was to curl up and sleep, forever. But I did start the next day.

It is hard to say how I was able to get through my first day and the days after that. It is as if I was operating on automatic pilot. But get through it I did and it became that bit easier with each passing day. And, even though it was clearly not the job for me, my employer gave me the idea to start my own computer training business, as he had been very impressed with my computer skills.

I put the idea to Maria and, true to form, she and Doney set up a training room for me at the back of their home and allowed me to use their side entrance for the students to come and go. The room was fabulous and within no time at all I was getting clients to come and learn to use the computer. It was very exciting, especially when the FÁS CES Supervisors started to send their employees to me. This was the beginning of a new life for me in business.

Maria had the most wonderful garden at the back of the cottage. You could go out the back door and up a narrow path onto the lawn. There were trees which provided shade against the hot summer sun and added a balmy air in the warm afternoons. It was a real little haven and she and Doney took great care of it. It was wonderful to sit and relax, to read a book or just chat to each other, or better yet, just sit and reflect. However, not even this tranquil environment could compensate for the problems that were to arise over the following months; events that could so easily have pushed me completely over the edge and led me to commit suicide.

I wasn't in Newcastle West long before I started to see the consultant. I rarely spent more than ten or more minutes with him after the initial interview. He passed me over to a psychologist, whose name escapes me. The psychologist urged me to write my story down and then if I wanted, burn it. I thought this to be a waste of time as I would only ever write my story if were to serve a better purpose than just getting everything off my chest.

I had told the consultant about my suicide attempt and he told me that he would have to sign me into a psychiatric ward for a minimum of three months, during which time I would be heavily sedated. I told him that this was not an option I was prepared to consider. He replied that I must at least give him a firm undertaking that I would not make another attempt to commit suicide and that I must agree to have my medication supervised. I told him honestly that I could not give him the undertaking as I was still suicidal. He made it clear that without such an undertaking and my unwillingness to consider sedation, that he was not prepared to prescribe me any more medication. I was left to battle my depression, anxiety attacks and suicidal tendencies alone. It was to be like climbing the tallest mountain naked and on my knees. It was truly awful, but I was determined to do it and I did.

Following the advice of a new psychiatrist, I left Maria's home in May 1996 and started a new life on my own. I was able to concentrate on building up my business, which I did with a fair degree of success. The business was doing so well I had to employ six people. We moved to much bigger premises, which meant I was able to expand the range of services I could provide and that we would have our own training rooms. The business was looking good and so was my future. It was a very positive time in my life and I was getting on very well with just about everyone. I was getting an increasing amount of business from FÁS and our presentation evenings were very well attended and well received. I'd commissioned a competition amongst the students on the Post-Leaving Cert course to design a business sign for me that would be in keeping with the town and the castle. It was a huge success, as was my involvement in the Knights of Desmond Festival. It was one the most successful ever and I was proud to be the chairman that year.

Everything was going great until September 1996 when Barbara called me and asked if I would travel to Dublin to meet her as there was something she wanted to ask me. I refused and insisted that she should travel to Limerick. She agreed and arrived a few days later. I really wish she hadn't.

Chapter 13

A Second Chance

Consuetude est altera natura
Habit is Second Nature
[AUCTORITATES ARISTOTELIS]

B arbara arrived in Limerick on a Wednesday and stayed over with me. The reason she came to see me was to say that she had made the most awful mistake and she pleaded with me to give her a second chance. To my eternal regret, I gave her that second chance and paid dearly for doing so.

We discussed the possibility of reconciliation over the next few weeks and I agreed to spend Christmas with her in Dublin. She seemed like someone who really had changed and who was anxious to make a go of things, and, if truth be told, I really felt sorry for her.

Our Christmas together was pleasant enough and Barbara certainly seemed to be on her best behaviour so that, slowly but surely, my resistance to giving her a second chance began to erode and it was increasingly difficult to say no. Before I left Dublin and returned to Limerick, I had made the decision to say 'yes' and to give her a second chance. In March 1997 she and our two dogs moved to Limerick and we began trying to rebuild our relationship.

We put the house in Dublin up for sale as I did not want to have any attachments to Dublin. Barbara eventually agreed.

On the day of completion of the sale, I made it absolutely clear to Barbara that if she changed her mind and didn't want to sell the house, to tell me, as I did not want her making a mistake. She assured me that she was happy to go ahead and so we signed the contracts and sold the house.

We divided what remained after clearing the mortgage between us and we were free to spend the money as we chose. I opted to invest it in the business. Barbara invested some of her money in the business, but unfortunately, she squandered a substantial part of it on drinking and smoking. All of this was to come back and haunt me later. And so it was that we left Dublin behind and moved to Limerick.

To help us get off to a positive start I booked a weekend in the Springfields guest house in Killarney, where we'd spent the first week of our honeymoon. I distinctly remember driving towards Castleisland with John Denver playing on the car cassette player. I had such terrible feelings of regret: I knew I'd made the most awful blunder in agreeing to try again with Barbara, but as I'd made it, I was determined to see it through.

For the first few months, things really did look like they were going to work out, but after the summer of 1997, Barbara was beginning to show all the signs of reverting to type. She became disinterested in me and began talking about how much she fancied one of my brothers. She later said that she regretted us getting back together. It was around October when I overheard her on the phone to her sister Mary, telling her that she had made a terrible mistake and that she should never have come to Limerick.

The months passed and I tried my damnedest to keep my new computer-training business going, while sinking further into the depression that engulfed me. We'd moved from

Newcastle West to a farmhouse in Rathfredagh, Co. Limerick, and for the first time in many years I came in contact with rats, who were living in our house. Barbara left the doors open for the dogs to come in and out at will, which, of course, was an open invitation to the rats; and they certainly took full advantage of the opportunity presented to them. I would come home from work late at night only to see the rats running into the house. While I tried to sit watching television, I would hear the rats in the kitchen and their droppings would be all over the kitchen table and worktops and in the drawers; everywhere really. No surprise then that I became increasingly ill and frequented my doctor with stomach and bowel problems, not to mention the ever-increasing stress and depression. I was reaping the whirlwind for having giving her a second chance.

Christmas 1997 was one of the stormiest for years and it knocked out the electricity around West Limerick. Ours was knocked out for five days, from Christmas Eve through most of Christmas. My neighbour Geraldine's mother very kindly prepared some Christmas dinner for us, which was much appreciated. We passed away the time playing games like Frustration and listening to the radio. Barbara and I talked a lot about the future and it was becoming obvious that Barbara had deep feelings of regret about coming to Limerick.

It was in early January that the whole truth finally emerged. She had been in contact with the home help supervisor, who informed her that she would receive all her benefits again if she was living alone. She told me this in a way that left no doubt as to what she wanted me to do. So I asked her straight out: 'Are you telling me that you want me to leave so you can get your benefits back?'

Her reply was short and very much to the point: 'Well, if you want to, you can, and it would mean I'd get my benefits back.' This felt hellish and I was at a loss as to what to do next. What is the point in trying to save a marriage where one person is so intent on ending it? I went around for days with my head in a spin. It didn't help that she was back talking with our Dublin neighbour, making it obvious that she missed him. In the following April she sent him a vulgar and very explicit birthday card. I was astounded and extremely upset. Here was I trying my best to make this marriage work, after *she* asked me for a second chance and she seemed to be indifferent. What was it going to take for me to cop myself on. I told her that I was going to look for a place of my own.

Just as it seemed that things couldn't get any more difficult with Barbara, I met Kathy, the mother of one of my employees, in April 1998. When I first met her, I was immediately impressed with her beauty and by her abilities. She was a true mother and homemaker and had all the qualities that were clearly missing in my own mother. She was also one of the most feminine women I'd ever met in my life and I very quickly found a place for her in my heart, which she holds to this day.

When I met Kathy I had no idea that she was going to have the most profound effect upon my life. It is no exaggeration to say that Kathy did more to help me develop a better sense of myself than any other person I'd ever met. I would visit her often and enjoyed her company immensely; we had many things in common and I felt we could be very good friends and companions, which I am proud to say is what we became.

When Barbara was introduced to Kathy and her family, she saw how well we got on and did everything she could to encourage it, for motives she was soon to reveal. I genuinely resented her attempts at encouraging me to have an affair with Kathy, as that is not at all what I was interested in, or, how I felt. When I challenged her behaviour she unashamedly disclosed that she was seeing someone else! To say I was gobsmacked would be an understatement. At the same time, I was learning more and more about Kathy's own unhappiness, and the more I learned, the more convinced I became that we were in the same boat, so to speak.

Events with Barbara were deteriorating so badly and my depression was worsening to such a degree that I felt I really needed to get away altogether and so decided not just to leave Barbara but to also leave west Limerick altogether and start over somewhere else. This decision was to result in some later difficulties, but moving away from west Limerick and from Barbara was to mark the end of my days as Thomas Dunne and open the way for me to finally emerge as the person I was always meant to be: Sara-Jane Cromwell. I am eternally in Kathy's debt for this.

I told Kathy of my decision to leave west Limerick, to which she replied that she, too, wanted to get away and have some time to herself to think about what she wanted to do with her life, so we started to look for a suitable place to go. While I was reading the *Irish Examiner*, I came across a business opportunity in Midleton. I asked Kathy if she would be interested in coming with me to look into it, and so we travelled to Midleton on a Saturday to meet the man who had placed the ad in the paper.

When we got to Midleton we took to it immediately. I had a meeting with the man who had the IT training room and also the landlord of a premises in the Rosehill Business Centre in Ballinacurra. I was on a high and felt very optimistic. No matter what had happened with the business opportunities, I was determined to make a fresh start and move to Midleton. I told Kathy of my decision and that she was welcome to join me and that we could share a place, to save on the expense of renting and to be company for each other while she decided what to do next. She thought about it for some time and came to the decision, entirely on her own, that she would come to Midleton with me and stay for about two to three weeks and then move to Birmingham to her sister, Stacy.

In moving into the same house, Kathy and I would lay ourselves open to rumour and accusation, but the truth of the matter is, we were two unhappy people whose friendship would sustain us through difficult times. And we remain friends to this day. It is entirely understandable that her family were deeply upset when she left Newcastle West. It is even understandable that they and her so-called friends misunderstood the true nature of our situation as it was then. It was Kathy's own decision to try and find a new life for herself; that was entirely her right and it should have been respected. I had heard of the vulgar comments and accusations being made about me, but I comforted myself with the truth and held steadfast to the fact that I knew how things really were.

Chapter 14
Midleton

Home, home, sweet, sweet home!
There's no place like home! There's no place
like home!
THE MAID OF MILAN [J.H. PAYNE]

When we moved to Midleton on 18 September 1998, I had a mere £800 at my disposal, which had to pay for food and the next month's rent. Our only other income was £160 per week from my own business in Newcastle West, which was expected to keep us both until that business was sold to one of my own employees.

I had been told just how hard it would be to do business in a small town like Midleton, and I would have to agree that it has proven tough at times. I won't lie and say that I never experienced difficulties, but for the most part I have been very well received in Midleton, so much so that I have made some wonderful friends, even amongst my clients.

Struggling with debt and with the stresses of the previous year beginning to take their toll, I wasn't long in Midleton before I tried to drown myself in the river that ran alongside our apartment. We had gone out for a drink with Kathy's son and his girlfriend. Something was said that upset me and so I left the restaurant and went for a walk. I really had no idea until then just how depressed and fragile I had become over the previous few months; something snapped that night which left me feeling utter despair. I just wanted it all to stop and so went down into the river. But as in the case of going into the sea at Lahinch, I realised how awful it would be for Kathy and so I left the river and went back to the apartment, only to be greeted there by two gardaí. I had been reported missing. Kathy must have sensed how bad I was and was worried about me enough to contact the gardaí out of concern for my wellbeing.

I decided to sell One-2-One Communications, my business in Newcastle West, to one of my employees and to set up a new business in Midleton under a different name; MetaCom Consultancy Services. I started as a sole trader, then invited Kathy to come on board and set up a limited company, which we did in early 1999. We provided training and consultancy services in a number of areas, concentrating on health and safety, and on computer training for groups and on a one-to-one basis. We advertised in the local papers and within no time we became very busy, but it would be a long time before we would see anything like adequate income coming in and our debts were mounting, so the financial stress began to tell.

The pressure from work was becoming so great that we had to decide on whether to move the business into an office premises in the town rather than operate it from our home. We found a place nearby and moved in, in November 1999. It turned out to be a disaster. When we returned from the Christmas break we found sewage stinking out the office, a problem that was to persist for the following five months, which meant that we had to bring the business back to our apartment.

Things looked up when we received our ECDL accreditation, but no sooner had we received the accreditation that would help us to get back on our feet, than we were told by our landlady that she was selling our rented apartment. We were completely devastated and stressed out. It did nothing but plunge me back into a deep depression and Kathy decided to go back to Limerick to stay. I was at my wit's end. So back to Limerick she went to try and sort herself out. I really couldn't blame her, but it hurt me terribly and it was the last straw.

Throughout this whole period, the ever-growing issue of my gender conflict was to take the most unexpected turn. While I was still living in Rathfredagh, Barbara, who had met Kathy, had shown her some of my clothing, but never explained its significance. This left Kathy feeling confused but she said nothing to me until we'd moved to Midleton. Kathy returned from Newcastle West one day and noticed that her dresses were hanging differently in the wardrobe, but wasn't exactly sure of the reason for it. Then there was an occasion when we were out shopping in Roches Stores in Limerick. Kathy saw me looking at a mannequin and becoming very distressed. She got the strange idea that I was going to attack the mannequin, which, of course, was an absurd idea, but she was absolutely right about me being distressed; how could I have been otherwise, given everything that was happening. I absolutely loved shopping with Kathy, but the downside was the frustration I felt every time we went shopping and I could not buy the clothes I really wanted to. Added to this was Kathy's correct observation that I showed little or no interest in men's clothes.

Kathy was convinced that I was eyeing up other women while we were out together. She noticed how I'd be looking at them while driving or walking about. She interpreted this as my fancying anything in a skirt. I found this very upsetting because nothing could have been further from the truth. What I was doing was looking at what women were wearing and picking up ideas on what and what not to wear for my height and shape etc.

Finally, after the incident with the mannequin, she questioned me about her clothes being rearranged. The time had come to confide in her about the problem I'd been having with my gender conflict or cross-dressing as I knew it at the time.

Why did I leave it so long to tell her? Because I wasn't sure if she was going to be staying around or if she was going to England to her sister and my situation was far too important and sensitive to be telling people about it, only to find myself alone because of it, the most terrifying thing for those who have to disclose their condition.

I finally plucked up the courage to tell Kathy of the lifetime I'd spent living with the stress of feeling like a woman in a man's body and my need to dress accordingly. I was about to do one of the most frightening things I've ever done in my life. What made it so terrifying was that I really enjoyed having Kathy around and what I was about to do could literally destroy our friendship forever, especially as I couldn't give a precise reason for why I felt this overwhelming sense of being in the wrong body. Like so many others, I didn't know the exact reason for feeling as I did, but I'd had a whole lifetime of experience living in the wrong body. What was happening now was about to change all that.

Kathy said she wanted to see what the dressing was about and suggested that I try on one of her dresses and use her make-up. She waited downstairs while I nervously dressed and put on my makeup. I didn't have a wig to wear and felt really weird and stressed. I had a sense of this being the moment of truth and a point of no return, regardless of how she reacted.

I came down the stairs, watching her reaction as I came into view. Her face said it all and it was evident that she was distressed by what she saw, but not for the reasons I'd imagined. I thought I looked liked like a freak to her, but she just saw a woman. I sat down and talked about how we were both feeling. Then she said something I thought I'd never hear in my life: 'You're definitely a woman and you need to do something about this. You'll have to go and see someone about this.' She also told me that she was very distressed at seeing a completely different person in front of her and that even my voice had changed and that she was scared, and she looked every bit of it, so I went and changed back into my own clothes.

It really is hard to say that the experience was in any way enjoyable, but it certainly marked the beginning of the end of my having to live in the wrong body. Kathy overcame her initial distress and, from that moment on, whenever we went shopping she would encourage me to buy clothes and we had some very funny moments when she spoke to me as just another of her girl friends. We would be looking at something and she would turn and say, 'You should get that, it would look really good on you.' The only problem was that other women would be standing close-by and would look over at us, wondering why she was talking to me like that. I would go red and nudge Kathy. She would say that she just felt natural about it.

The more we shopped, the more clothes I bought and I began to dress more frequently. Whenever Kathy was away and we spoke by phone, she would ask me if I was dressed. I would ask her how she knew: 'Because your voice always changes.' I honestly hadn't realised that and it made me think about what would happen if I lived every day of my life as the woman I felt inside. I didn't dress every day as that would have been impractical, but I did every chance I got and it felt more comfortable every time.

During this period I made the decision to go back to work as a sole trader and kept the business name. I was doing personal development courses for FÁS Community Employment Schemes. It was during these courses that people noticed certain telling female traits coming through. As I discussed various issues regarding relationships, it was very obvious where I stood: the women on my course were at a loss to understand how I knew so much about being a woman and this struck them as extremely odd. Never once during these courses did I ever let on about my gender conflict, but that didn't stop them from noticing and questioning my motives.

I remember two instances in particular. One was a course I taught in Ennis, Co. Clare. As the course progressed, the women began to question how I knew so much about being a woman. I couldn't explain it to them other than to say it came from experience, which was partly true, but how could I explain the rest of it when I didn't fully understand it myself; it was just second nature to me. I remember receiving a cake and a massive-sized thank-you card signed by everyone who had done the course. One of the ladies wrote: 'keep something for yourself'. As it turns out, she was a counsellor and so would have known if I was merely bull-shitting everyone.

The second instance was a health and safety course I taught in Mitchelstown for the female staff of a well-known local paper. One of the course modules was manual handling. As part of the demonstration, I had to show the women the incorrect way to lift loads. Women have a very different method of lifting to men: the locked-knees method and the side-and-twist method. They are distinctly feminine in nature and are completely different from the way in which men lift. There is simply no mistaking the difference and you really have to be a woman to lift a certain way. When I was demonstrating the incorrect method to the ladies, one of them literally said: 'Is there something you want to tell us, Tom?' I immediately replied with a very red face, 'Yes, but not right now.' Ultimately, when my disclosure was made, I understand that there was a lot of delight amongst some of these women, because they had known that something was different about me that now finally made sense.

Before I got to this point, however, I would have to go lower than I ever had before. On two occasions, I took an overdose of tablets and downed a lot of alcohol. The simple fact was that I wasn't able to cope with the strain my situation was putting on my friendship with Kathy and the constant stress from trying to earn a living while having to deal with Barbara's resistance to my application for an annulment to our marriage.

I felt extremely fortunate to have someone as strong as Kathy with me. She was clearly very distressed and very angry at my suicide attempts, but she did not understand the depth of my distress and the depression I was under. As a man I was expected to be the strong one all the time but that really was impossible and unsustainable, not least because I was really a woman, and a very sensitive one at that, trying with increasing difficulty to be the man I was expected to be. What mattered was that I get on with trying to run my business so I could keep a roof over our heads and food on the table.

The whole situation was getting to Kathy and brought her to breaking point. Her husband had died and she was feeling very torn between wanting a new life and missing her children. She didn't need to cope with my situation; something had to give and it did. Kathy returned to Limerick and once again I was on my own.

I honestly could not see any way through the seemingly endless difficulties, so suicide once again seemed like the only way out. Of course it was not, but when you reach such a low point and all around you seems utterly dark and hopeless, you see suicide as a relief to those you leave behind. I decided to end my life, believing that I wouldn't be missed by anyone, especially not by my family.

On a Sunday afternoon, I made myself ready. I did try to contact Kathy in the hope of telling her how I was feeling and that she might be able to offer me some comfort, but she was not answering her phone and in my sensitive state of mind I thought it was because she didn't want to talk to me. I decided to make a success of it this time. What I didn't know as I downed the tablets and the whiskey was that Kathy was actually on her way back to Midleton with her daughter and her daughter's boyfriend. They arrived at the apartment only to find me in a semi-conscious state. I was taken by ambulance to the Mercy hospital. Even in my condition I was able to see how angry Kathy was and how she'd had enough of my persistent efforts to try to kill myself.

I was kept in overnight for observation and Kathy was to collect me around lunchtime. I slept right through to the morning and when I awoke spent the entire morning pondering what I'd done. Clearly, I was not meant to die, and there must be a purpose to my life. I thought of all the reasons why I felt so bad and so depressed and came to the conclusion that I had to stop seeking approval from everyone around me by living a false life. I finally started to accept that I could not go on living as a man and that I was going to have to find the courage and determination to do something about it. I didn't have a clue where to start, but start I must. It was with this new resolve that I went home to Midleton. It was to be another two or more years before I finally got to see Dr Kelly, but I did and I have never looked back since.

I spent the intervening period building my business and dealing with my depression. I did not seek medical intervention as I did not believe I had a clinical depression. There is no doubting that, once I made my decision never to attempt suicide again, I found an inner determination and strength to see it through. I decided to put a plan in place to build a new life for myself and I started by giving Kathy all the reassurances I could that I would never put her through that kind of distress again and took every step necessary to fulfil that promise, and I have kept it to the letter. Another of my plans was to develop a much more positive state of being, both in mind and body, and to rebuild my health and wellbeing. This involved making contact with my parents in order to give them one last chance to reconcile with me and if they didn't, then it was going to be fine: I was determined not to keep carrying the hurt on my shoulders and in my heart.

A radio interview with Ger McLoughlin at the RTÉ studios in Cork helped me immensely at this time. Describing me as a very gentle and kind man, the interview was about how I was struggling to deal with my depression without the help of medication or psychiatric intervention, as I was absolutely certain that my depression was not clinically related. This decision helped me to realise that, in my depression, I was on a journey of discovery and my perception changed from one of fear and dread to one of purpose and determination.

It was in this much more positive state of mind that I resolved to look for the help I needed to deal with my gender problem and to remain steadfast in my belief that my marriage should be annulled; nothing else was going to do me now. I resolved to use my suicide attempts for the good of myself and of others. I used them as a barometer of the true nature and extent of my own difficulties: nothing could bring me as low again as when I was sitting on that hospital bed alone.

The defining moment came when I went onto the internet and typed in words like, 'transgendered', 'transsexual', 'cross-dressing' and 'Ireland'. The result was a number of e-groups that offered support for people with gender problems. Among the contact names, one was Diane Hughes, who gave me the name of Dr James Kelly, a psychologist specialising in gender identity cases, and his phone number in Dublin.

I started to dress more frequently but still hadn't made an appointment with Dr Kelly, partly due to my business keeping me very busy and the whole situation with the annulment of my marriage to Barbara. The Legal Aid Board had finally assigned me a solicitor to deal with my application for nullity and so I was busy preparing discoveries and affidavits. We also had to move house a couple of times during this period, from Willowbank to Castlemartyr.

It was while in Willowbank that I secured a two-year contract as Associate Faculty Lecturer with the National College of Ireland. This came completely out of the blue when I was asked to replace another lecturer at short notice. In spite of having very little time to prepare my lectures, all of my students got through their assignments successfully, and I received excellent feedback from the college, which pleased me greatly. Later on, I was offered a contract with the college on the strength of the work I'd done and on the strength of my résumé. The next year I was given another contract. Things were definitely looking up.

When I received news that I was to get a contract, Kathy and I decided to go to the Midleton Park Hotel to celebrate. We discussed so many things that night, but one subject really stands out and that was the name I should go by if I decided to go ahead and live as a woman. Up to that time I had preferred the name Jenny, but Kathy felt that the name did not suit me and that Sara-Jane suited me a lot better. I agreed and felt that she had given me a very precious gift. Her support had meant the world to me and so it was a terrible loss to me when she returned to live in Limerick. But she was with me when I first went to see Dr Kelly and later when I stepped out for the first time as Sara.

Chapter 15
Being Myself

And above all these things to thine own
self be true
HAMLET [SHAKESPEARE]

It was August 2003 and I was driving to Dublin full of apprehension and excitement. I was finally going to get to the heart of why I felt so much like a woman and why I needed to dress as a woman — to *be* a woman. I had often thought that all of this was due to some maladjustment during puberty and adolescence and that it had something to do with my sexuality and my inability to determine whether I was heterosexual, gay or bi-sexual. I was open to whatever Dr Kelly had to tell me and was very happy to resolve the situation for once and for all, especially if it meant finally coming to terms with my need to be and dress as a woman. This was a really big deal and I had a sense that all those years of praying and fasting were to be answered for once and for all.

Dr Kelly took me by surprise with his rather conservative views on the issues we discussed, but he also gave me a lot of reassurance. I felt secure in whatever he had to tell me and I was genuinely prepared to be told that my problem was nothing more than a compulsion to cross-dress. I wanted to put this all behind me and move on with my life. But in order for that to happen I had to be absolutely honest with him.

I told him that I was cross-dressing and that I felt it could be because of a maladjusted adolescence. I was open to finding out the reason and to getting whatever help I could to resolve the matter. Then I said, 'But if you were to ask me how I really feel, then I would have to say that I really feel like a woman on the inside.'

Dr Kelly suggested we start at the beginning and asked about my family background and history and so on. As time went on, my body language changed completely as did my voice and I was so relaxed that my female personality came out, despite all my efforts to keep it hidden. Dr Kelly told me that he would have to carry out a second evaluation before he could give me a diagnosis. I had to return in a couple of weeks and it was some wait. I spent the whole time imagining what Dr Kelly was going to say to me and how my life was going to be affected thereafter. I tried to imagine him telling me that I was woman in a man's body and where that news would take me, not the least being any decisions I might have to make about gender reassignment and what it would entail.

So I returned to see Dr Kelly, but this time I was alone, which was probably just as well, given the enormity of the news I was to receive and my need to take it in. Dr Kelly made it clear that there was no doubt in his mind that I had a female gender identity. I was just a woman who happened to be born into the wrong body, and all because of something that happened within weeks of my being conceived. I'm not a freak or a mental case, I had a real condition, Gender Identity Disorder.

No sooner did I get my diagnosis than I was discussing being referred to Dr Donal O'Shea, the Endocrinologist at St Colmcille's hospital in Loughlinstown, to commence my hormone treatment and the gender reassignment process. I was also to undergo a second psychiatric evaluation to confirm Dr Kelly's diagnosis. But there was one other very important matter: I was required to come as Sara on my next visit to Dr Kelly. Oh, my god, I thought. It is one thing to know yourself to be a woman trapped in the wrong body and to long for nothing more that to be set free to live your life as you have spent a lifetime imagining it, but it is quite another to actually dress fully as that woman and go out in public. But everything I'd been through over my lifetime was pointing to taking this step and, to be honest about it, I was completely determined. I asked Kathy if she would come with me and she agreed. I was so happy and appreciative of her being with me and it gave me the courage I needed to go through with it.

My next visit to Dr Kelly took place on a clammy November day and I could hardly sleep the night before between the excitement and the terror. I got up about 5.30 a.m. and got myself ready. I had breakfast but could hardly eat it on account of being so nervous. I took one last look in the mirror before leaving and when I did, I was rooted to the spot. Of all the times I'd dressed and put on my make-up, they were never like this one occasion. This was me going out into the world as Sara for the very first time. I had to do everything I could not to burst into tears. I felt like my new life was about to start.

We left for Dublin about 7.30 a.m. but not until after I'd made numerous trips to the toilet. The only good thing about the journey was being in my car, but it was warm and sweaty. I normally make one stop on the way to Dublin, but this time I had to stop about five times.

We eventually reached Dublin. Heading towards Capel Street Bridge, my nerves were shattered, but I was bursting to go to the toilet again and so we went down to the toilets in the Jervis shopping centre. I had been so nervous imagining what could happen to me, but I hadn't thought that my first culture shock as a woman would be having to wait in a queue to use the women's toilets. Only one young teenager looked at me, which I thought was very strange, as I had expected more curiosity. I know that this is going to sound strange, but, while I sat in that cubicle, I felt like I really belonged and it felt peaceful. But when I stepped outside again, I was in a complete panic and rushed out of the toilets and told Kathy I needed to get back to the car.

Kathy suggested that we go for a walk as this would give me the chance to calm down and relax before going into Dr Kelly. So we did, but not before I put on my long grey coat and hat. We walked along the boardwalk on the Liffey. As we headed back towards the car, a man was walking towards us and he seemed to be saying something. Of course, I thought he had sussed me and was saying something rude, but as he got nearer he looked straight at me and said: 'I was just saying to myself that you're a very lovely looking lady.'

'Oh, my gosh! Oh, my gosh!' is all I could say in response, while Kathy said: 'There you are now, and there was you wondering what people would think.'

It was five minutes past four and we headed for Dr Kelly's office. I went in ahead of Kathy and when I entered Dr Kelly's office, he just kept looking at me as if I was a total stranger.

'Hi there, sorry I'm late,' I said.

He just kept looking at me and said, 'I'm sorry but I am expecting someone else but their appointment isn't until half-four.' It was at this time that Kathy came through the door and the penny dropped. 'Is that you Sara?' I confirmed that it was in fact me and thanked him for not recognising me and said that I must be getting off to a good start. He told me that I looked very impressive and very passable even at that early stage of my gender reassignment, and that he had no advice to give me about my dressing or my make-up.

Then, Dr Kelly proceeded to take me through the various stages of my reassignment, one of which was that I would have to have a tracheal shave, that is, have my Adam's apple shaved to give me a female shape to my neck. But I don't have an Adam's apple and he was very surprised about this. He said it was going to be a significant advantage going forward.

He then asked Kathy how she felt about it all, to which she replied that it was my life, but that she couldn't understand why as a woman I would still be looking at other women. Dr Kelly explained that it is perfectly normal for women to look at other women, especially as women always compare themselves to other women — what they wear, their hair, their figures etc — and that it was entirely natural for me as a woman, even trapped inside a man's body, to be making the same comparisons and trying to imagine what it would be like to look like those women.

He also tried to explain that my gender identity had nothing to do with my sexuality. I was delighted to let him say all this as I'd been trying to explain all this to her myself. She had been listening to all kinds of opinions from her friends and acquaintances in Limerick, who, though they knew nothing about my condition or situation, were telling her that I was just doing this for sex; that I was gay and that I wasn't prepared to admit it. She also had to listen to other vulgar and disgusting remarks which can't have been nice and which are unrepeatable here.

I got to see Donal O'Shea, the endocrinologist, in February and was referred on to Dr James Lucey at St Patrick's

Hospital in Inchicore. I had to see Dr Lucey for a second psychiatric diagnosis before I would be allowed go onto hormone treatment and start the reassignment process. I met Dr Lucey's colleague, a woman, initially, who was very warm and pleasant and, though the assessment was very difficult emotionally, she made it less stressful than it could otherwise have been.

The longer the assessment went on, the more emotional I became and cried quite a bit. The whole situation was overwhelming for me. The doctor was amazed at the transformation taking place in front of her eyes as once again my body language and voice changed, which is what usually happened once I didn't have to hide my true gender from people. She was in no doubt as to the soundness of my diagnosis and so went in to speak to Dr Lucey. She was gone a while and I used the time trying to contemplate the various stages of the process still in front of me and whether I would have the courage to see it through, especially when I imagined the treatment I was likely to receive from my friends, my clients and from strangers.

Dr Lucey arrived in with the doctor who had assessed me to tell me that, based on the information I had given, he would have no problem confirming Dr Kelly's diagnosis. Then he asked me a strange question: 'Would you not think of staying as you are and not going ahead with having a reassignment surgery?' I immediately responded by saying that I hadn't come all this way not to complete my reassignment. He then asked me how I felt at the prospect of losing my genitals. Again my response was immediate. I told him I couldn't wait to have the body I knew I should have had since I was a child and that nothing would be allowed to dissuade me from that. He seemed pleased. He then said, 'I wish you the very best, Sara, you have a very interesting journey ahead of you.'

The meeting with Dr Lucey and his colleague was extremely difficult and I was emotionally and mentally exhausted from it, but I also felt that I had achieved something monumental in demonstrating my determination to see all of this through. I was prepared to put myself through these gruelling evaluations to do it, even if it meant constantly retelling my history and having to recount the long years of abuse and of feeling like a freak. It was really hard, but it was so worth it to get to that stage of my journey towards being myself. Every single stage of this process was proving to be difficult and a test of my resolve. There were so many reasons I could have given for deciding not to go ahead, but to give up would have been to deny myself of my true *self*, and that was a fate worse than death.

In making their diagnoses, Dr Kelly and Dr Lucey had to consider the possibility of what are called *contra-indications*. These are other possible explanations for my persistent sense of being a woman in a man's body. For example, they had to look at the possibility of a maladjusted adolescence, a failure to come to terms with my sexuality or over-exposure to female company and influences. Then there was the need to consider the possibility of fetish tendencies, such as cross-dressing and transvestism. In the case of Dr Lucey, he had to look at the possibility of psychiatric disorders that could lead me mistakenly to believe myself to be a female born into the wrong body. Once they had satisfied themselves that these had been safely eliminated then they were able to make their diagnosis of gender identity disorder.

It is extremely important to remember that a person presenting for a diagnosis of GID must have at least two years of persistent discomfort living in the role of the opposite gender and demonstrate that the disorder is the only possible explanation. This was a no-brainer in my case as I have had this throughout my life.

On Thursday 20 June 2004 I returned to Dr Donal O'Shea, only this time I was coming away with my first ever prescription for hormones. Dr O'Shea advised me that I would become very emotional and experience mood swings as a result of taking the hormones. I told him that I was already very emotional in a female kind of way. It was good for a laugh.

I was started on Premarin (oestregen) and Aspirin, to stop my blood from clotting. I started on the lowest dosage of Premarin for a number of months in order to allow my body to get used to it. A few months later I was prescribed twice the dose, which I remained on for about a year. It was a surprise to find I'd reached normal female hormone levels over such a short time. I did notice, though, some time after I started the Premarin, that my palpitations returned for the first time in many years. This made me wonder about the connection between the palpitations I'd suffered during my adolescence and my monthly breakouts of female acne, and if this was a result of having higher-than-normal levels of female hormones back then.

Now, I'm at the second-last stage of my reassignment, before surgery, and have been put onto an anti-androgen known as Zoladex, to kill off any remaining testosterone in my body, which I take as an injection into my tummy, just below my navel. The needle is about two inches in length and I have opted to inject myself because it means avoiding long waits in my doctor's surgery and it also helps to keep my costs down. Gender reassignment is hugely expensive and most of us can ill afford it. One of the major effects of

Zoladex is that it significantly reduces my libido, which, quite frankly, is a great blessing. This is extremely important to me as it shows that going through gender reassignment is not a sexual matter. Another benefit of Zoladex is that it softens the skin and facial features. These changes have been noticed by many people I know and has given me great confidence in how I look.

Of course, one of the biggest benefits is the fact that my breasts are now growing. Thirty-three years I've waited for this; thirty-three years before my body could feel in some way normal. And it is one of the most joyful things in the world to me and makes me long for the final stage of my transition even more; my genital realignment surgery. As I'm at the second-last stage of my gender reassignment, I have just one more step before I will be forever free of the term GID and everything related to it. I have seen the surgery being performed and what happens afterwards for those who have undergone the operation. It is hard to express the sheer joy and ecstasy that flows through me just at the thought that that will be me one day, hopefully in 2008.

Thinking about the final step in my transition, I have had to consider where to go to have my genital realignment surgery carried out. As things stand, I have three options, being referred to Charing Cross in London, to Leicester General or Thailand. Going to Thailand means going private, and though it is not as expensive as going to the UK, it is still quite expensive. Also, there are very serious risks in travelling so far away for such major surgery, especially if there were to be any post-surgical complications. There are no post-surgical supports here in Ireland for people who go to Thailand for their surgeries. I've seen first-hand what can happen when someone goes that far away, especially when they have not thought it through. Going the to the UK is much slower and involves having to go through a whole lot more evaluation and re-evaluation, which can be very distressing and discouraging for those who have already gone through the evaluation process here in Ireland. However, I find it very reassuring that they are so meticulous about it, ensuring that people are certain about what they are doing. For me, there is absolutely no doubt, but I recognise that the process has to be thorough, despite the frustrations. Given my public role in raising awareness and wanting to encourage people with the condition to act responsibly in getting the best possible care, it has been important for me to set a good example throughout my own transition, which I hope will become a role model for others to follow.

One of the major steps in gender reassignment is to live every day in my female gender role. And as much as I may want it, it is extraordinarily scary. Going out in public, going to work every day and meeting my clients and explaining my situation to them; shopping; meeting my friends; meeting strangers; all that potential for stress, panic attacks and completely freaking out. There are plenty of reasons to give up and to revert to living as a male, but what a horrible thought; it's enough to make me want to stay a woman!

One of the key pain barriers to cross in gender reassignment is removal of facial hair by laser treatment. It is so painful and not for the faint-hearted. I had my whole face done each time and the results have been worth all the pain and burning, not to mention looking like a Martian with green Aloe Vera gel spread over my face. I looked quite the sight stopping at traffic lights, with other drivers looking in at my green face. I just hummed away to myself, delighted that I had withstood yet another torture session.

Buying clothes was tricky and it was really great having Kathy come with me and to advise me on what did and didn't look right on me. Most of my shopping was done in Evans and Marks & Spencer's, as they sell to the larger-sized lady. They are also friendly towards people with GID. I was size 24–26 when I started out and was determined to get my weight down, which I've managed to do; so much so that I'm able to buy my clothes from high-street boutiques. I've come down to size 16–18 and am aiming towards size 16, which is ideal for my 6.75 feet in height.

Chapter 16
The Outcast

Against stupidity, the very gods fight
un-victorious
LETTERS AND SPEECHES OF OLIVER CROMWELL
[THOMAS CARLYLE]

Another huge milestone for those of us with gender identity disorder is telling our families and friends about it and having to cope with their reactions. It can be hard for them to understand that the disorder is a congenital condition and not a lifestyle choice or a fetish.

I first told my family about my condition in April 2003, but my disclosure was the culmination of more than a year of phone calls and a difficult family meeting about the abuse that had taken place when we were children. At this stage, after many years of having little or no contact with my parents, I had begun a series of phone conversations with them, trying to get my mother to acknowledge that she had been wrong to believe for so long that I was 'retarded'. To me, these phone conversations were make-or-break, and I was delighted when they apologised. I really thought, or wanted to believe, that they had changed.

Christmas 2002 was to prove one of the most momentous events in our family's troubled history. I received several phone calls from my brothers and sisters telling me that there had been some angry scenes in my parents' home over the

Christmas and as a consequence a family meeting was being held in Co. Wexford, where they now lived. I was welcome to come down and express my feelings about what our parents had done to us.

I made it clear that I had already started the process of reconciliation with them and that I was making progress (as I thought) and that my reason for going to the meeting would be to confront the rest of my family over the way they, too, had treated me over the years. They agreed that I should be able to do that and encouraged me to attend. The meeting was held early in January and was attended by most of the family. Two of my siblings stayed away. I was determined to use this opportunity to try and get closure on the various issues I had with my brothers and sisters.

I sat on the sofa, between a brother and sister. My eldest brother opened the meeting, explaining recent events and the need for the family to confront our parents over their treatment of us. My mother tried to make out that were ganging up on them and that this was wrong, but her tone and body language betrayed her attempts to put us on a guilt-trip from the off. It didn't work, so one by one we expressed how we felt about our treatment over the years. It truly was a momentous event and even I had my eyes opened by some of the honest revelations that came from my brothers and sisters. I was the second-last to speak and made it clear how I felt about their treatment of me. This was followed by an acknowledgement from every brother and sister present that their behaviour towards me had been wrong and inexcusable and that they would make sure never to repeat it again. I really thought I had finally received closure and reconciliation with my family, so much so that it influenced my next major decision, to disclose the situation with my gender conflict.

I travelled to Wexford a number of times after the family meeting. Each visit seemed to indicate that things had indeed improved between us and between my brothers and sisters. I spoke regularly to some of my sisters, albeit I was the one doing the calling, but the conversations were friendly and led to my going to visit some of them.

I phoned my mother and asked if I could come down to visit, as there was something I needed to tell her and Dad. It was arranged for me to travel down with Kathy on a Sunday in April 2003. I brought some photographs I'd had taken while we were on holiday in Salou, my first holiday with Kathy where photographs were taken of me as Sara-Jane. I was extremely nervous driving to Wexford that Sunday morning and it was a great comfort to have Kathy with me.

We had a lovely lunch with my parents and the atmosphere was convivial and conducive to sharing my situation with them. I started by telling them about how I'd always found it difficult to live as a boy growing up and that I had been dressing as a woman as that was how I really felt myself to be inside. I then showed them the photographs of me as Sara, as I was calling myself when in female mode. They were shocked at the news and even more so when they saw the pictures. They said I looked like my younger sisters. Then my father poured wine into our glasses and stood up and toasted my courage and wished me every happiness for the future.

I was deliriously happy and felt absolutely that I had done the right thing in telling them. They even thanked me for trusting them and confiding in them. My father and Kathy went onto the patio and left me and my mother to talk in the dining room. We had a very open and frank discussion about whether she should tell my brothers and sisters. She said that she would keep my secret, but I told her I had nothing to hide and that I'd prefer it if she told them. So it was agreed that they would be told over the coming days.

Initially, there was a mixed reaction to my disclosure by my brothers and sisters, but it was positive for the most part. In fact, most of them promised to come and visit me in Cork and even suggested having a party to celebrate having a new daughter and sister. I was on such a high during those few months. By the end of 2003 at least four of my siblings had met me and had been really impressed with, and supportive of, my transformation. Three of them were openly declaring their support and one invited me to her wedding, as Sara! I had travelled from Cork to Portlaoise and to Cavan to visit my sisters and a brother in order to introduce them to Sara. They were undoubtedly nerve-wracking experiences but they were so worthwhile.

The last family function I attended before my sister's wedding was my mother's 70th birthday party. I was still living as Tom and just getting used to my new situation. The party was a nice occasion and everyone seemed happy to meet me. Some of my brothers told me they were going to be the same towards me as they were when I was Tom, which included being vulgar. I told them I didn't mind so long as it was based on acceptance. Surely now, for the first time I could truly feel like I belonged to this family?

It was now eighteen months since they had been told of my condition, and numerous expressions of support had been given along with promises to come and see me and an invitation to my sister's wedding in December 2004. It would not be hard to imagine, therefore, the utter devastation when I discovered that they meant none of it and that, despite being well advanced into my transition, I would be asked by my sister to attend her wedding as a man! How did all this come about? Two words: *my mother.*

All the time she was letting on to be supportive of me she was making it abundantly clear to my brothers and sisters that she had no intention of ever accepting me as Sara-Jane. She had me as a son and that was that; never mind the fact that she told me in the most shameless manner that she never wanted me, always resented having me and resented my being so different as a child. Her initial support when I had visited with Kathy had really been just for show — she hadn't wanted to be embarrassed in front of my friend. Of course, my brothers and sisters would do anything rather than go against our mother, so, in spite of all their outward professions of support, some of my siblings began privately to refer to me as clown and a freak while some of my other brothers and sisters would even try to persuade me to change my mind and not go ahead with my gender reassignment.

It was in late 2003 or early 2004 that I was invited up to my sister Martina's house and told that my closest brother, Peter, was coming down to see me, ostensibly to meet me and for me to explain my condition to him, in order to give him a better understanding of it; that it was going to be a friendly and supportive experience, but it would not turn out that way at all. I had been in Martina's house a while when Peter phoned to say that he was on his way and he wanted to know if I was dressed in women's clothes, because if I was, then he wasn't going to come down. Martina assured him that I wasn't dressed in women's clothes and so he agreed to travel down. He eventually arrived at the house, but before he came in he looked through the window to check that I wasn't dressed.

My brother then began a provocative rant about a sensitive subject in what I know was a deliberate attempt to goad me in order to make a point about my false claims (as he saw it) of being a woman born into the wrong body. The more I resisted his attempts, the more agitated he became until I thought his head would explode, so I stopped the argument by asking him why, after not seeing each other for so long, he would choose to behave in such a manner. He shocked me with his response: 'To prove that there's no fuckin' way that yer a fuckin' woman!'

I was completely gobsmacked. 'Are you for real?' I asked him.

'Yes,' he said, and he was deadly serious.

'And how do you make that out?' I asked.

'Because there's no fuckin' way that woman could be as fuckin logical as you are.'

I burst into laugher at such a ridiculous assertion and turned to my sister to see her reaction. She was clearly shocked by what she'd heard.

'So, let me see if I've got this right. You're saying that I can't possibly be a woman because I'm too intelligent?'

His answer was immediate and as clear as could be. 'Yes, that's exactly what I'm saying and, if you don't like it, then tough fuckin' shit.'

The penny was finally dropping for me. I asked Peter if he was trying to prove that I wasn't a woman and if this was the real reason for his coming to meet me in Martina's house, to try and talk me out of going ahead with my gender reassignment. He said that this was correct. I then asked him if he was aware of just how offensive this was to me and how terribly hurtful.

Again he was as clear as could be: 'I don't give a fuckin' bollocks if you're offended, just get fuckin' over it.' The only thing more frightening right then than Peter's hostility was the realisation that I had been set up by these two and quite possibly by the rest of my family and that these were the two who had volunteered to be the ones to carry out the plan to get me to change my mind. As if my condition was nothing more than a state of mind.

I left the house and walked around the town in the early hours of the morning and in freezing cold weather. The question going round and round in my head was: how many more of them are involved in this setup? Are my parents involved? If they are, that means they are not really accepting me despite leading me to think that they are. So how many of my brothers and sisters have also been lying to me? I determined to return to the house and put these questions to them.

But as soon as I returned, Peter apologised profusely for his outburst, justifying it on the grounds that he was nervous and wasn't sure how to handle it. I accepted his explanation.

Martina opened a rare bottle of Spanish liqueur, saying it was a special night. She had the pictures of me as Sara that had been sent to her earlier and we showed these to Peter. This was the first time he had seen them and could see right away that this had nothing to do with my being a transvestite or cross-dresser. He was also shown pictures of the different hypothalamuses and he said that seeing them helped to make sense of my condition. We spent the rest of the night and the early hours reminiscing about the past and Martina told me how proud she felt whenever we talked on the phone and how she used to tell her husband how eloquent I was. My hope returned, for a little while at least.

However, in spite of such moments, another eighteen months were to pass and, despite travelling long distances to meet some of them and putting myself through the stress of meeting them as Sara, not one of them phoned me during that whole period to see how I was, to arrange to come and visit as they had promised or to express even the slightest concern for me. Any conversations that did take place by phone were the ones I'd initiated and when I did call, I tried not to talk too long about my situation and made it my business to enquire into how things were with them. Eventually, I thought I would bring them all up to date on my progress and so wrote to each of them. I enclosed an up-to-date photograph that had been taken during a photo shoot for a feature in the *Irish Examiner* and a leaflet that explained GID. I expressed my disappointment that none of them had come to see me as they had promised and hoped that I would get to meet them soon. I also requested that they call me Sara from that moment on. I then received a number of phone calls in which I was accused of putting the family under pressure! I couldn't believe my ears. This was around August and September 2004.

Come October, matters became irretrievably bad. I'd received a very unpleasant and upsetting letter from one brother in which he made it clear that, not only was he not prepared to accept or to respect my request to be called Sara, but that he would call me any kind of vulgar name he chose, 'except Sara, until I'm ready'. I was doubly hurt because this brother had more reason to treat me better for all the times I'd stood by him through his many difficulties. He even wanted the name of my consultant so he could question him about my condition. He demanded this as a condition of accepting my diagnosis.

I received a number of phone calls from members of my family during this time, saying that there was a problem with me going to my sister's wedding as Sara. I was told that there were concerns about what might be said to me or about me on the day and that I might be upset and that it might be better for me to go as Tom. I was shocked and tried to reassure them all that I could not see a problem and that I was perfectly capable of looking after myself. I then received other calls in which I was told that some of my brothers and sisters were saying that I would look like a side show at the wedding and that people would be laughing at me. They were clearly together in this with my mother.

Their desire that I should attend the wedding as a man rather than a woman completely and deliberately ignored the simple fact that I was by now looking far more feminine than masculine, not to mention the fact that my breasts were growing and would have stuck out through my shirt. Everything about me was feminine and there was no way that I could have gone back to being a man. But this was completely ignored by them.

It all came to a head when my sister phoned me personally and asked me to attend her wedding as a man and to wear a suit. This was to become a pivotal moment for me and them. I realised that my family had not changed at all in its attitude towards me and that it was imperative for me now to move on and to have nothing more to do with them. It would have been so easy to justify becoming bitter towards them, but I was determined not to. Never again would I allow them to bring me back to that place where I'd tried to end my life; never again.

But the biggest test of my determination still lay in front of me. The last time I had spoken to my mother was during the whole wedding débâcle. I was very honest with her about how I felt about the way she and my family had treated me and that I found the whole thing an act of betrayal by all concerned. I challenged her to give me one good reason why she was not prepared to meet me; she had none. I really was hurt and decided not to have any further contact for the foreseeable future, save to keep my promise to find a suitable wedding gift for my sister as I'd promised. She told me she'd like an angel, so I searched high and low for months before I found the right one. It was an angel with its wings covering a child to protect it.

It was ten o'clock on Friday 23 September 2005 and I was sitting at my office desk working. The phone rang and it was my father on the other end of the line sounding very distressed. 'Thomas, I'm afraid I've some bad news, your mam died this morning at half-eight.' He went on to tell me that she had had a major asthma attack and that she had not responded to her ventilator. He told me how he tried unsuccessfully to apply CPR. She died in his arms.

It is hard to describe the effect of this news on me. I had been grieving for the loss of my mother for over twenty years and now she was finally gone for good. She died without accepting me as her own, just as she had failed to do throughout my entire life. I felt the most incredibly sublime peace and knew immediately that I would not be going to the wake or to the funeral. I wanted to be left alone and come to terms with the realisation that she could never hurt me again, ever.

At about 11.30 a.m. I received a phone call from my youngest sister Sophie who wanted to know if I'd heard the news and to know how I was. She then asked if I was going down to Wexford, to which I replied that I would not.

'Well, she was still your mother, Thomas.' I told her I did not wish to discuss it further and wished her well, but she insisted that I should go down. I replied by telling her that I was not going to be a hypocrite and pretend to grieve for someone who had treated me so badly right up to her death. 'Well, I think you're wrong.' She handed the phone over to Graham, who also tried to convince me to go down, but again I refused.

He said: 'We know you had your differences but she did love you. I know she loved you.' I couldn't agree.

The next call I received was from my brother James. Had he heard right, I wasn't going to Wexford to say goodbye? I repeated that I wouldn't be going, to which he replied: 'You mean you're not going to your own mother's funeral?' I simply replied that I had my reasons for not going and that I really did not want to talk about it. He just said, 'Good luck so,' and hung up.

When I got up on Saturday morning I noticed a missed call on my phone. It was from another sister, Brenda, saying they were concerned for me, that they loved me and that she would call back later on that day. She never did. In fact this was to be the last time I spoke to any of them until Friday 3 November 2006 when my sister called me as I was driving onto the M50.

I could barely hear her, so didn't recognise her voice at first. She eventually came through clearer and told me why she was phoning me. She was calling out of respect to tell me that the gardaí in Ballyfermot would be contacting me to take another statement about what I knew of my sisters being abused by our father. 'Sweet Jesus' was my response, followed by a long pause and I really struggled to come up with a response. On the one hand, I really didn't want to be talking to any Dunne and I was shocked to be hearing that the case against their father had been re-opened. I say 'their father' because, just like their mother, he was certainly no father to me. Shortly afterwards two garda detectives came back and took a second statement from me.

Since first writing this chapter, I've been contacted by two of my sisters and a brother, who want to re-establish their relationship with me. In fact, I've already met my two sisters and understand that a third also wants to make contact with me.

When I met my sisters Sophie and Clare it was a wonderful and loving experience and demonstrated the utter futility of the divisions and distance that had been between us. We had very open and honest conversations about the various issues that divided us and the fact that I'd been so shamefully treated by my entire family. The girls accepted this fully and apologised to me not once but several times over. I have to admit to having been suspicious about why they wanted to meet me after all this time, but they have since demonstrated how genuine they are, with Sophie and her husband travelling all the way from Cavan to see me. And I even got to have a life-long dream come true: to have a real girlie time with my sister Clare as we hung out together on her sofa in our pyjamas watching movies and drinking wine. It was every bit as wonderful as I'd always imagined it would be.

My brother Peter heard about my appearance on TV3's *Ireland AM* programme, and that I'd looked very well, and told me that he wanted to meet me. He had spoken to my sisters and had been shocked to learn the extent of the lies told about me over the years. He now seems to want to put matters right between us. He concluded one conversation over the phone by telling me: 'Sara-Jane, you don't have an evil bone in your body and you never did anything to any of us.' Peter is now helping me to get some photos for this book and we're trying to arrange a meeting to see if we can re-establish some sort of relationship in the future. It feels wonderful to have a family again. This is the way it should always have been and hopefully will be from now on.

Chapter 17
Annulment

The court doth make an order declaring:
That the purported marriage between the
Applicant and Respondent...was and is null and
void and of no legal effect.

Monday June 26 2006 was a red letter day by anyone's standards. It was my birthday and I could easily think of other places I would rather have been, but here I was again, hoping that it would be the last time I would appear in court on this issue; my application for an annulment to my marriage. It was like something you'd see in a movie. For years Barbara and her solicitors had pursued me for maintenance, and thus, an admission of sorts that a valid marriage had existed, but I was resolute that that was not the case and for several very good reasons.

Barbara delayed a hearing for my nullity application for years and put me through several discoveries, which were not granted by the courts. I had given seven years of accounts and yet still they pursued me and tried to stall the hearing for my application. They were relentless in their efforts to pursue a judicial separation, and I was equally adamant that I wanted an annulment. It was heartbreaking to think that after all that she had put me through, she could get away with this too. However, I was determined to see this through, even if I had to do it myself. Thankfully, I didn't.

In March of 2006 I was informed by my solicitor that I would have to prepare yet another Affidavit of Means. I was distraught and went into a complete tiz. *Here we bloody well go again.* It was really hard to take and there were times when it crossed my mind to go the judicial separation route, but I was determined to see this through to the end. I had always felt that right was on my side. I was unshakable in my conviction, even though it would have been far easier to get a divorce. But, as much as I hated having to admit it, I knew that I was never truly married and I needed vindication after all the lies and bad treatment.

In February 2005 I had written to my solicitor to inform him of my diagnosis and my decision to go ahead with gender reassignment. He told me that this would affect my application for nullity and that I would need confirmation from Dr Lucey by way of a report for the court. So, I returned to see Dr Lucey for another assessment as his office has misplaced my original evaluation. During the meeting he made it clear how impressed he was with my transformation since the last time he had met me.

On the day of my court hearing I arrived as Sara. I was as nervous as could be and just wanted the case to be heard and get out of there as quickly as possible. I felt extremely self-conscious and vulnerable as this was the first time my legal team were meeting me as Sara, as would Barbara and her legal guardian and legal team, not to mention the judge and everyone else in the courtroom. I sat in one of the consultation rooms with the court-appointed psychiatrist, Dr Draper, and we were left hanging around waiting for Barbara to arrive, only to be told that she wasn't coming and that the hearing would not now go ahead. I was livid and at the same time plunged into more despair. I was convinced that this was going to go on forever. I was so dejected returning to Cork, but I had to pick myself up and keep going; not an easy thing to do, but do it I must.

However, there was one positive thing to come out of these events and that was receiving the reports from Dr Lucey and Dr Draper. Bearing in mind everything I'd been through and all the stigma, bullying and abuse I had been exposed to over my lifetime as a result of being branded a mental retard and a freak, their reports would have a profound impact upon me.

Dr Draper wrote:

Findings:
(S)he presented as a well-dressed attractive female. (S)He had laser treatment to remove facial hair and a very female complexion and soft skin. (S)he feels that (her)his health is improved and (her)his depression and stress is lessened, (S)he has no suicidal thoughts and now has a strong sense of self. The transition has been very positive for (her)him. (S)he made a lot of friends. (S)he is writing a book on gender dysphoria. (S)he plans to change (her)his name by Deed Poll after (her)his case has been heard, (S)he appeared to be very relaxed in (her)his role as Sara and displayed predominantly female traits...(S)he did not want to be a cross-dresser as it is not a pleasure thing...

Opinion:
It is my opinion that because of (her)his lifelong female gender identification it would have been impossible for (her)him to enter into and sustain a normal heterosexual marriage...

Dr Lucey wrote:

On mental state examination she was a tall, pleasant woman wearing an auburn wig and purple eye shadow. Her speech was fluent, coherent with NO RETARDATION *and no psycho-motor alteration. Her symptoms were confined to issues in relation to her gender identification. There was no evidence of psychosis, no panic, anxiety, no phobia,* NO COGNITIVE IMPAIRMENT. *Her mood was normothymic.*

In summary, Sara (Thomas) Dunne is a 45-year-old woman with gender identity disorder. Born as a male, Thomas Dunne, she has been attending a personal psychotherapist since 2003 in relation to gender identity disorder and has been on long-term steroid hormone replacement therapy for that condition. She has multiple life stresses and a disturbed personal background. She acknowledges that she did not reveal these details to the court-appointed psychiatrist in the past. These factors do need to be taken into account when considering the validity of her marriage contract.

In a nutshell, I am a perfectly normal woman who happens to be tall and attractive and, I did not have a valid marriage contract. But most importantly of all for me, I am not, nor ever have been, a *mental retard*. I had to wait forty years to see this in writing and I've cried many tears over those words. It would have been nice had my mother just said, 'Sara, I'm sorry for letting on that you were mentally retarded.' She never did and she never will, but my psychiatrists did and put it in writing for the court to see

On 26 June 2006, my birthday, twenty-five years of unmitigated marital misery were to end after just twenty minutes in court. After all the delays, I was told on the Friday before the court hearing that they were prepared to withdraw their objections to my application for nullity.

And so it was that my case finally got underway with Dr Draper being called to the witness box. Before he was called, the judge questioned why I'd changed my name to Cromwell; to which my barrister responded that it was my right to choose whatever name I liked and that the court was bound to accept it. The judge was quick to assure my barrister that he was not commenting one way or the other, that he was just curious about the name. The hearing proceeded and Dr Draper was called as a witness. I was genuinely shocked to learn of his credentials and to realise that I had such an esteemed witness giving evidence on my behalf.

The judge asked him if I could simply say I was gender dysphoric for the purposes of getting an annulment, then revert to being a male afterwards? Dr Draper could not have been more emphatic in his response: he made it absolutely clear that my condition was medical, that it was a prenatal condition and that it could not be cured. The judge was completely satisfied and said that he was prepared to grant my application, providing there was no objection from Barbara's legal counsel. She stood up and said that there was no objection and that there were no other applications before the court; with that the judge declared that the marriage was annulled.

It is very difficult to describe how I felt at that moment. Here I was, Sara Cromwell, whose name had just been changed by Deed Poll, who had only been living six months full-time as a woman, experiencing serious financial difficulties and trying to cope with the daily trials of starting a whole new life, and being single into the bargain. I could only wonder what kind of a life awaited me when I left that court-room for the last time.

Chapter 18

Going Public

Truth demands a response
[GAIL PETERS]

There was never a single doubt in my heart and mind about making a public disclosure of my condition. Was I afraid? Absolutely; actually, afraid doesn't cover it; I was genuinely terrified. Such a disclosure could easily blow up in my face. There was a lot to lose if it went wrong, but there was so much more to lose if I didn't tell the truth. Hiding away was never going to be a long-term option for me. Yes, there were a great many days when I hid behind my front door and was afraid to go out, but I used those occasions to work through my fears and then step out once and for all. It occurred to me that some real good might come of all this and that there was no other Irish person in mainstream society who was doing what I was about to do. There were some who were doing it on the fringes, but that is not where I and many like me wanted to live, so someone had to do it if we ever to get our medical condition out there and to stop apologising for it. So rather than ask the usual question: *why me?* I chose to ask another question: why not me? and why should I leave it to someone else to speak up for me? It really was that simple for me.

Even before I had received my diagnosis, I was fully aware of society's ignorance of gender identity disorder and the treatment of those struggling to live according to their true gender identity. I was aware of the fact that sensationalist TV shows and tabloid newspapers portrayed such people as a bunch of freaks and ultimately reinforced the confusion and prejudice that surrounds this medical condition.

I knew all this before I was diagnosed and before I chose to proceed with my gender reassignment. I was aware of the accusations of deceit and selfishness made about those of us who try to live as we were meant to live; normal lives within our families, places of work, communities and within society as a whole, but in their true gender. I was also aware of how some families could be more concerned about their own embarrassment than about doing the right thing by those they professed to love. They find it hard to understand and accept that GID is a congenital condition, affecting the brain and that a person with GID simply cannot reconfigure their brain structure and psychological make-up to conform to their body. And this really is the simple truth of the matter. To quote Prof. Louis Gooren: 'It is the body that has to change in order to match the imprinted gender identity.' There is simply no other way around this, unless one wants to live in a state of interminable and intolerable conflict with one's self and with everyone else. I have chosen to live my life freely, and not to hide who I am and who I was meant to be.

It is against this background and the fact that there was no support organisation of any kind to help people with GID that I felt I had to go public with my condition, in the hope that the truth of my situation would help me through my own transition and would also help those coming after me. There are large numbers of people with gender identity disorder who, like I did, suffer deep distress and depression and many have either seriously considered or tried to commit suicide.

In March 2004 I moved into my new home in Midleton. I can still remember the overwhelming sense of dread I felt. Kathy was happy to live in this area of the town, but I now had to face into my transition in a neighbourhood in which I knew no-one and there were lots of children and teenagers about. Moving outside of town was my preferred option because of the highly sensitive, and to be brutally honest about it, the terrifying, prospect of transitioning towards my true gender. I wanted to live somewhere that would allow me to come and go quietly without attracting the possible ridicule and judgmentalism that others in my situation were experiencing at that time. It seemed an entirely reasonable strategy to adopt. But, no sooner had I committed to the move than I received my wake-up call: *Jesus, what am I going to do now about my transition?* I found myself in a dilemma and needed to work it out fairly quickly.

One of the options I considered was to defer my transition indefinitely, which would have been intolerable and heartbreaking in equal measure, while the other was to try to keep my head down as best I could and let on that there were two tall people living in the house, one male and one female! Another mad idea we came up with was for us to go to Spain to complete my full gender reassignment then come back as Sara. The only problem with this rather silly idea was that Kathy would then have to explain what had happened to Tom and who was the woman who came back with her? I know, I know, it was really silly, but this situation can do that to you sometimes.

However, I need not have worried. I decided upon a different course altogether and that was to allow a certain time to pass in which I would try to get to know my neighbours and give them the opportunity to get to know me, as a normal person like themselves; as someone who just wanted to live in peace and get on with my life. Thankfully, I got to know my immediate neighbours in a very short period of time. This gave me the confidence to approach them individually and to explain my situation in an open and frank way. I put together an information pack which I then used to explain my condition to them.

Once I had decided to tell them, I approached all my immediate neighbours and explained my condition and what was going to transpire over the following months. They admitted that they were shocked and did not understand the condition, but they expressed their gratitude to me for telling them and wished me well. Others told me to tell them if I ever needed anything. I gave them permission to tell my other neighbours, as they were then likely to get a more accurate insight into what was happening. I was dumbfounded by their kindness and acceptance, which has made all the difference to me, and undoubtedly helped me to overcome some of my worst fears. I can honestly say that I have never felt as safe anywhere in my entire life. They exemplify the best of what good neighbours should be.

Hardly had I told my next-door neighbour and her daughters, than I was made welcome into their home and treated like one of the family. One of the girls was fascinated with the whole thing and would come to my defence whenever she heard her friends and schoolmates saying anything nasty about me. We share the same shoe size and it has been a running joke that Victoria has larger feet than me!

Shortly after I made my disclosure to my neighbours I was invited to a girls-only night in one of my neighbour's, Gail's, home. She invited me because she immediately identified with me as Sara. I did not dress on that occasion as I had not yet met one or two of the neighbours and I didn't want them to feel awkward. It proved to be the right decision. The girls made me feel completely relaxed and never once did they say or do anything to make me feel awkward or embarrassed.

One of my neighbours told me that her family thought I was one of a couple who just happened to be tall and who were working shift work. She said how they felt sorry for *us* as it must have been difficult for us to be coming and going at different times. I was chuffed to hear that and couldn't help laughing, just as I do every time people call to the door and want to know if my husband is home. There have been times when a few of the men asked if I had a husband and when I said I hadn't, wanted to give me their phone numbers.

I was calling to one of my clients, Conny Ovesen, in Robinwood Furniture, one afternoon in around June or July on some business matter, and while I was there I was introduced to Alice de la Cour of the *Irish Examiner*. Conny encouraged me to tell Alice about my situation; Conny had found the whole thing fascinating and thought I was very courageous to have told her and others about it. She actually felt proud to know me and so encouraged me to tell Alice. Alice asked me if I would be interested in doing an interview for the *Irish Examiner*. I said I would if it was handled sensitively and in good taste, being extremely mindful of my friends, neighbours, clients etc.

Alice was as good as her word and I was contacted some days later by a journalist, Helen O'Callaghan. We agreed to do the interview on 29 July. I waited anxiously and without any idea of what I was going to say, but once we got started, I relaxed, and the interview went on for a considerable time. Towards the end Helen asked if she could confess something to me. I said 'sure' and so she told me that when she was thinking about meeting me she wasn't sure if she'd remember to call me Sara and whether she would be comfortable. But she said that when she'd arrived all she saw was a tall, elegant lady. I was chuffed and went red.

On Wednesday 4 August the photographer from the *Irish Examiner* came to take photographs to be included in the article. I was feeling very awkward at having to pose for the camera, but hey, it had to be done. I then received a phone call on the Friday afternoon. It was Alice de la Cour: 'Sara, if you don't mind my saying, I've seen the photographs and, to be honest, they don't do you justice.'

I was taken aback but before I got a chance to reply Alice said, 'Sara, would you mind if I spoke to my editor and arranged for you to have a makeover? I can't help feeling there is a beautiful woman in there bursting to get out and I want to help her to do that. Would you mind if I look around and get you some outfits that I think will suit you better than the one you're wearing in those photos?' I was absolutely thrilled and not a little red-faced. I agreed to her proposal and we both finished the call very happy and excited about doing the makeover. Me, getting a makeover? I was euphoric, like the cat that got the cream.

On the following Monday, Alice arrived at my house with three outfits, fashion jewellery and make-up, all of which were given on loan from Andrew Thomas Jewellers on North Main Street and Unicare Pharmacy and Evans on Patrick Street. Gail was with me during the makeover and she was completely amazed at the transformation taking place in front of her. Alice made me over from head to toe and it was exhilarating. I remember when she was putting on my eye shadow and suddenly jerked backwards and said, 'Jesus girl, I'm starting to fancy you meself. You're competition for me now, so you better stay away from my patch.' That did my heart a great deal of good. We were just finishing the makeover when Conny arrived with a bouquet of flowers, a bottle of champagne and a fabulous cake, which was for after the photo-shoot.

The owner of the Water Rock restaurant, Tom Cleere, kindly agreed to let us use the lovely grounds for the shoot. When I arrived I had no idea that my friend Tricia was on duty. As I came out of the kitchen she came out from the bar and stared straight at me and asked if she could help me. She didn't recognise me for a few seconds until I indicated that it was me. She was completely shocked and delighted at the same time and after the photo shoot was finished I got her and Conny to get into some photos with me. It was a truly wonderful experience. We returned to the house and had a girlie night in devouring the cake and the champagne.

I also did interviews that year with the *Sunday Observer*, BBC Radio Scotland, Cork 103FM and RTÉ's *The Big Bite*. One aspect of disclosing my condition that made me very unhappy has been the way people automatically assume they could ask me questions about my sex life and my sexuality. Some have been quite crude, especially those men who would say things like, 'Jaysus girl, you have great balls to do what you're doing. I know I certainly couldn't do it in a million years.' To which I would immediately respond: 'Not any more I don't.'

People would ask me if I'm heterosexual, lesbian or bi-sexual. The simple truth is that I'm sexually ambiguous to asexual and have very little interest in that particular aspect of my life. There are far more important things for me to think about. It is a simple matter of fact that my sex drive is virtu-ally non-existent at this point in time and will be for quite some time to come, with no guarantee that it will ever return.

I knew that this could happen once I started on my hormone treatment and happily accepted it as a price to be paid in order to achieve my lifetime's dream of being a woman; of being Sara. And in all truthfulness it is quite a liberating experience, as it frees me to focus on more important issues, like raising awareness of this condition and the sorry state of things for those of us born with it, through no fault of our own.

I've also had my fair share of smirking, ridicule, speaking behind hands, nudges, name-calling, filthy remarks about me behind my back, people trying to avoid me and so on, but all they've done is reinforce the reality of who I truly *am* and my absolute determination to be true to myself and everyone else. I refuse to be put down by these people or allow them to frighten me into giving up. I am blessed with more than enough friends and supporters, who'll make sure that I don't ever go back to those dark days.

Life was going on throughout all these events and some lives were coming to an end. In May of that year Kathy's sister Nell died from cancer. This was a life-changing experience for me as I was present when Nell passed away. Nell and her husband Tony had returned to Ireland to retire, having lived in England for many years. Nell had been taken into the Mercy Hospital for some tests and Tony came to stay with us for a few days, then Nell's daughters came and, rather than have them separated in a strange city, myself and Kathy offered to put them up. They stayed with us for a few days and, during that time, they were told that Nell's cancer had become terminal. It was arranged to have Nell return to England, where she would receive palliative care. All the arrangements were made and Nell was due to travel to England within the next few days and, despite the expected outcome, there was a sense of relief that she would be amongst her loved ones during the last few weeks of her life, but regrettably that is not how things worked out.

On Sunday morning at around a quarter to five we received a phone call from the hospital asking us to go up as Nell had taken a turn for the worse and was not responding to treatment. We arrived around half-five and found numerous doctors and nurses trying to bring Nell's blood pressure back up and for a while it looked as if they had succeeded. Unfortunately, though, there were other complications and her situation continued to deteriorate to the point where they gave up trying. To relieve her pain, Nell was allowed to control her own morphine drip.

Nell clearly knew that she was reaching the end of her time and so began to prepare herself to say goodbye to her family. Her deterioration was more noticeable by the minute and it could be seen in her demeanour that she was fully accepting of it. She took the rings off her fingers and placed them in a mahogany box, along with some other personal items, she then handed them to her husband who sat by her bed, trembling at the prospect of what was to come. The doctors came back to the ward and called Tony senior and junior to one side in order to explain what was happening and, rather than leave Nell on her own, I went over to her bedside and held her hand and stroked her hair with my other hand. Then her daughters in England were informed of what was happening so the phones were handed to Nell. The expressions of love and the sounds of goodbye through the phone lines where absolutely heart-wrenching. Nell was dying during these calls and another daughter was talking to Nell's daughter-in-law in an adjoining room.

Within moments Nell began her slow graceful descent into her long sleep and as she did so, I went to tell her daughter-in-law: 'it's time' I said, as she sat full of tears, trying to tell her sister-in-law who was so far away, that her mother was in the process of dying as they spoke. One can only imagine the scenes on the other end of the phone. We returned to the ward and sat and watched as Nell slowly, effortlessly and peacefully slipped away.

It is an extraordinary thing to think that I had only ever met Nell twice before, it was in her home in Listowel. Kathy had told Nell about my situation and Nell replied that she worked with people who were in the same situation and found them to be very nice people to work with. She then asked Kathy what she should call me the next time she met me. Her acceptance of me has always meant a great deal, and so I was delighted to offer some hospitality to her husband and children during their time of great distress and to be there with her and be a comfort to her in those final moments of her life. It was an immense privilege.

A few weeks later I was to learn that one of my favourite aunts had passed away. My aunt Carmel, whom I dearly loved, and who was only ever loving and kind to me, was gone. I received a phone call to tell me she had passed away and what the funeral arrangements were. The funeral Mass took place in the Church of the Assumption in Ballyfermot and she was buried later on in Palmerstown Cemetery. There was a reception afterwards in the CIE Social Club in Coldcut. I was asked to sing in her honour and so I sang two of her favourite songs, 'The First of May' and the 'Fields of Athenry', after which I asked everyone to raise their glasses in her honour. My uncle Tommy and cousin Anthony were very touched by this and came over and hugged me.

*

2004 was proving to be a remarkable year for me and I find it surprising after so many years of difficulty, just how much I achieved in that one year. Not only had I gone public through the newspapers and radio, there were still more momentous events waiting to occur. It seemed as if destiny had well and truly intervened in my life and taken me to places and events that I simply would never have imagined.

One of the most momentous events for me that year was the founding of the first support organisation in Ireland for people with gender identity disorder. I invited a number of people to my home with a view to setting up an organisation to be known as Transgender Equality Network Ireland. The name was originally created by Diane Hughes and Dr Nicholas Krievenko, who devised the name during their submissions on the Nexus Report, which had been commissioned by the Equality Authority. However, the original name they went under was Transsexual Equality Network Ireland. The purpose of the Nexus Report was to examine the then situation regarding access to healthcare services for people dealing with gender conflict and those who had been diagnosed with GID.

The inaugural meeting took place in July of 2004 and the first committee was established. I was appointed as PRO and later on as Co-Chair. My vision for this organisation was that it should be an all-inclusive organisation for people with GID and their families. Our primary aims were to be a voice for those suffering in isolation and raising awareness about the true nature of the condition and for the urgent need for an adequate healthcare service and for legal recognition for those who were going through Gender Reassignment. I cannot go into all the details here, but suffice it to say there was nothing like this before in Ireland. This was a landmark achievement albeit with humble beginnings. From TENI, I founded GIDI, Gender Identity Disorder Ireland, which is doing extremely well in achieving my original vision for people with GID.

In my work with TENI and GIDI, a number of very significant and worthwhile projects on behalf of people with GID were initiated, including the first ever medical symposium on GID to be held in this country in collaboration with the Equality Authority, the HSE, the Department of Health and Children, TENI and GIDI; the introduction of an ID card system for those going through transition; meeting with representatives from the Garda training college in Templemore with a view to introducing a gender identity module into the curriculum, not to mention the many other projects on which I'm currently working.

After a while, I told my colleagues that I was finished with my involvement in GID matters for the moment, as I just wanted to get on with my life and focus on my genital realignment surgery, which will take place in Charing Cross Hospital some time in 2008–9, and on getting my business back on track so I could earn a decent living. But they asked me to a person to stay on and continue the work I'd started; that they felt I was the best person for the job and for driving things forward, and that they would support me if I decided to continue my work under another name. Ultimately, I made my decision to continue my work in GIDI.

I have disassociated myself from TENI, as I felt that organisation's decision to include all manner of fetish lifestyles which had absolutely nothing to do with Gender Identity Disorder was misleading. I feel that they are confusing the issue by using terminology that is outdated and no longer recognised as appropriate or helpful, and on using terms 'transsexual' and 'transgender' only serves to perpetuate mis-understanding and prejudice.

I have never made any secret of my dislike and opposition to the continued use of the terminology and therefore have completely disassociated myself and GIDI from its use, except only to clarify the difference between it and the medical terms gender identity disorder and gender dysphoria. This is a battle still to be won, but like all the battles I've ever fought, I'll stick at it until I win the day not just for myself, but for all those coming after me. If that can be my legacy having gone through this journey, the greater acceptance by society of those born with this condition, then it will have all been worthwhile. All of this has caused me to postpone the completion of my own transition, but it is time, now, to take care of it and bring it to completion, while not forgetting the purpose for which I fight.

The next momentous event of this year was an interview for the British *Observer on Sunday*, during the US presidential campaign — we actually came before George Bush and John Kerry, which was quite bizarre. It was Friday 15 October when Nicholas Krievenko and I met the journalists and photo-grapher in the Front Lounge on Parliament Street in Dublin. It was only my second time out in public and I was genuinely a complete bag of nerves. They were amazed to hear it and told me I looked fabulous; every compliment gratefully received. We had lunch and as I was not driving I had a couple of glasses of wine, which was just what I needed to relax, and believe me it was welcome.

While we were being interviewed the photographer came along and said she needed to take the photographs quickly as she had to be somewhere else. We got up to go with her thinking that she would take them there and then, but as luck would have it, she wanted to take the photos on the Millennium Bridge, down by the Liffey. 'For fuck's sake,' I muttered under my breath. I was mad, because I was so uncomfortable with the idea of having to walk down to the bridge then stand there posing, knowing that hundreds of people would be passing by and in their curiosity stare at us. I mean, this really was only my second time out! But I decided to just grin and bear it as best I could, get it over and done with and get back to a much-needed glass of wine, or two.

As we stood on the bridge the photographer had us pose in different positions. I was beginning to feel like a shagging model and, as expected, people did stare at us. To make matters worse, there was a strong wind blowing down the Liffey and I was terrified that my wig might fly off into the waters below; so I had to hold onto it, but in such a way that it looked like I was giving a girlie curl with my fingers. We eventually finished taking the photos on the bridge and much to my chagrin she wanted to take more, only this time along the streets in Temple Bar. She had us walk up and down the street and engage in conversation, as if we were oblivious to the camera and the people looking on; fat chance of that. I just decided that if we were going to be doing this in front of all these onlookers then we might as well have some fun and so I started telling Nick some funny stories which led to us both having a good laugh and that's the picture that ended up in the paper that Sunday.

Later that same evening Nick took me to a sushi bar. It was my first time to go to one and I have to say that the food was only delicious. When we left and made our way to get a taxi, I was approached by a man who asked me if I'd like to go for a drink with him. Of course I declined, but I was chuffed silly.

The next day we attended a conference of the Law Society, to review the first year of the enactment of the Human Rights Act. It was a who's who of the legal profession from Ireland, Northern Ireland and England. Nick wanted us to go up the auditorium and sit somewhere in the middle, but I was having none of it as I would need to go to the toilet quite a bit. He very graciously acceded to my request and so we sat at the back of the auditorium throughout the entire day. There were several hundred people there that day and I surprised myself with how easily I settled into the occasion. I felt I was amongst friends. Some of the speakers included the Lord Chief Justice of Northern Ireland, Baroness Kennedy from the UK and our own William Binchy amongst others; some of whom had been sitting alongside me during the course of the day and with whom I shared some humorous exchanges.

When we returned to our seats after lunch who should we run into but David Norris. Nick introduced us to each other. It was a very nice moment. I would meet David again at the launch in Outhouse of the confidential Garda advice service for the gay and lesbian community. David was one of the special guests and I was sitting in the audience. I went up to him to say hello and said, 'You might not remember me as it's about two years ago now…' With that, he said, 'Of course I remember you my dear, and isn't it very pretty you are looking too.' That man really does know how to charm a lady!

I returned to Cork on the Sunday evening, elated with my sense of achievement. To sit amongst that many people was just incredible and it emboldened me to do something else that I had been dreading; go down the town and buy myself a bottle of wine. I went down to O'Donovan's off-licence and as I went to pay for the wine, who should be serving me but Warren, the son of one of my friends, Roisín. He asked me how I was and what I'd done for the weekend, so I told him about the conference and the newspaper interview. As the conversation went on I was wondering if he recognised me, so I came out and asked him, 'Do you know who I am?'

He responded: 'Yes, of course, you're Sara. Can I say something and I hope you won't be offended?'

I told him to go ahead and say what he wanted to say and he did: 'I was just thinking that you make a very pretty woman and you look a lot better now than when you were a man.' I was so delighted with what he said and went red with embarrassment. I then went home and put my feet up and reflected over my glass of wine about all the momentous events that had taken place over that weekend.

Part of my job as PRO of TENI as I was then, was to seek opportunities for raising awareness about GID. With that in mind, I made contact with the *Big Bite* show, by e-mail. I wrote to them asking if they would consider doing a segment on GID and the plight of people with the condition living in Ireland. I received a very quick response from Zoe Liston, who said they would love to do a segment and asked if I could forward more details. My original thinking was that there were enough people to go and do the interview and that I would not need to go myself, but I would still have been doing my job by setting it up. I sent Zoe details of the people she could contact and invite onto the programme. But to my surprise, Zoe came back to me and said they really wanted to do my story as I was the one who contacted them in the first instance. She also asked me if I could get others to go along and be interviewed. I asked Lynda Sheridan, a colleague in TENI, who in turn asked her daughter Aisling, and I asked Nick Krievenko as he was a female to male. They all agreed as did my clinical psychologist, Dr James Kelly.

When I arrived at the studio I was greeted by Zoe and brought up to the hospitality suite. I was the last to arrive and when I did I found Nick and Dr Kelly discussing how they thought the issues should be addressed and who should answer what questions and in what order. But when they tried to share their ideas with Zoe she stated that the format of the questions was already decided and that I was to be asked the first few questions as I was the one who contacted the show. I felt strange about this as I was more than happy to defer to my colleagues. In fact, when we were brought into the studio I deliberately walked behind everyone in order to allow them to pick their seats, knowing that some would want to sit alongside David McWilliams. But as we approached the seating area we were placed in our pre-assigned seats; mine was beside David on his right, while Lynda was placed on his left side. The interview lasted about half an hour and it went very well.

When we'd finished I was approached by a number of the production staff who shook my hand and told me they really enjoyed the show and felt it was one of the best they had ever done. As I was leaving the studio I was approached by the producer, who thanked me for contacting the show. She said they felt honoured and privileged that I had trusted them with my story and that she hoped they'd done it justice. I assured them that they had. David McWilliams must have said goodbye to me about five times that day. Just as I was leaving, Zoe approached me to tell me the whole team were delighted with us and that I should contact them if there were any further developments. I mentioned in passing that I was thinking of writing my autobiography and a book on the subject of GID. She was very interested and asked if I had anyone to publish it. I told her I hadn't and wouldn't know where to start. She gave me the name of a publicist and told me that I was to mention her name when speaking to him.

I cannot commend the production team at the *Big Bite* enough for the courtesy and consideration with which they treated me and the encouragement this gave me to keep going. I had started this year and our new organisation without the slightest idea where it would take me. Nothing could have prepared me for the journey; even now I look back in wonder at what I've achieved. It was these achievements and the loving support of my friends that made me realise that I was reaching the point of no return.

Chapter 19
No Going Back

Often the struggler has given up,
When she might have lifted the victor's cup,
And learnt too late when the night came down,
How close she was to the golden crown!
Success is failure turned inside out,
So stick to the fight when you're hardest hit,
It's when things seem worst when you must not quit!
[DON'T QUIT]

D espite all the positive things that have occurred in my life since I went public about my gender identity disorder, there have also been many downs, some so great that they could easily have overwhelmed me to the point where I could have gone backwards into my old life, regardless of how awful that life was. I had to find a way of coping with my setbacks, discouragements and stresses in order to find the motivation and courage to keep going towards my ultimate goal: of having my body aligned to my internal gender identity. So I chose to make my suicide attempts my companions for the remainder of my journey. They are my constant reminder of how bad things used to be and of how far I have come and how much I've achieved since my last suicide attempt nearly seven years ago. Yes, it's been hard, bloody hard, but I did it and for the most part on my own, because that is ultimately how it had to be. But to move towards my full gender reassignment surgery I still had a number of steps to take. One of these was to change my legal identity, my name. Only then could I truly say I am Sara Cromwell and only then could I ever have the hope of finally living my life as ordinarily as everyone else.

I gave the go-ahead to my solicitors to take care of my deed poll in March of 2006. It should only have taken about two weeks to complete it and have it sworn in the High Court, but it took three months before I could finally and legally call myself Sara Cromwell. I finally managed to collect it a week before I was due in court for my nullity hearing. It was a momentous day for me as it was the most tangible affirmation of my commitment to see my transition through to the end. The next thing to do was change all my documents, legal and academic. This was a long and tedious process and is still ongoing. I've changed my driving licence, passport, car registration, motor tax, motor insurance, life assurance, pension, credit union, credit cards, bank accounts, medical records, PPS details, Revenue details, DPS card, accreditations, business stationary etc.; in other words, everything that had my old name on it. And it had its problems. Due to the delays in receiving my car registration and car insurance my motor tax ran out and I ended up being fined for non-display of a tax disc!

One of the highlights in changing my accreditations was returning my Diploma to the National College of Ireland with a request that I be allowed to go to the college to have new photographs taken of my conferral, as Sara-Jane Cromwell. I received the most lovely letter from a girl named Fiona, in it she invited me to visit the college in October 2007 when the conferrals would take place, that I would be provided with a cap and gown and a photographer would be made available to take new photos of me and my new Diploma. This is not untypical of the kinds of responses I've received. It has been the same when dealing with the Revenue Commissioners, the Motor Tax Office and the Passport Office. Through all of these interactions I've found the people I've been dealing with to be very professional, courteous and willing to assist me in any way they could.

Apart from being on hormones, the laser treatment to remove my facial hair has now left me with clear skin, which looks and feels lovely and soft and feminine. So, between the hormones and the laser treatment, I have become very feminine looking in my face. This is hugely important for passing as a woman and as it has let me down in the past; it feels great to have so many people recognise me as just another woman. This is extremely important for obvious reasons, such as using public toilets, women's changing rooms, being stopped by the gardaí and so on. The things the rest of society never has to think about.

When I started on my transition towards becoming Sara on the outside as well as on the inside I had to get rid of all my male clothes; all of them. There could be no holding back in case I changed my mind. Because having them would have been a crutch I could fall back on and that would have been disastrous for me. Getting my weight down was another major challenge. For health reasons and in order to be as passable as possible, I made it my business to lose as much weight as possible and to reach the weight most suited to my height. This means I can now go and buy my clothes in the same high street boutiques as everyone else, which has helped me a lot in overcoming the temptation to go back into my male clothes. One day, just out of curiosity, I tried on some of my male clothes and not a single one of them fitted me any more. I had such a laugh over it and decided then and there to finally get rid of them. It was an incredibly scary but at the same time a liberating experience.

Whilst going public has undoubtedly helped me enormously to stay the course there were still other major challenges I had to face and two in particular: going to work and travelling abroad. From the earliest period of my diagnosis I had told a small number of my clients about my situation, while others read about me through the different articles that had been published in the newspapers. In particular, I want to acknowledge all the folks at MHC Shopfitters who were absolutely fantastic and made it so much easier to cope with going to work as Sara for the first time.

Shortly after I told Karen and Ivan Nixon about my situation, I had to go into their workshop to carry out a safety audit inspection and a few weeks later I had to do a health and safety course for their employees. It was a Friday and I was a total bag of nerves. I was trying to decide what outfit to wear. I felt very self-conscious in a skirt, but then thought better of it. I thought, 'Sod this, if I'm going to do this then I'm going to look as feminine and professional as I possibly can,' so I wore my black-and-blueberry pinstriped suit and a blueberry coloured blouse. I also wore tights and court shoes.

I arrived at the Water Rock training centre feeling very nervous. Kathy very kindly agreed to come along for the day as moral support. She told me during the first coffee break that I looked and sounded completely natural and that there wasn't even a hint of maleness. She said she could not get over how natural and professional I was considering the immense pressure and stress I must have been under and she wondered how I could possibly have been nervous to begin with. She wasn't wrong about that as there were definite moments when I really wanted to run out of the place, but I never once let on about how I was really feeling and didn't want people feeling sorry for me. I had to get past my nervousness if I was to have any hope making a successful transition with my clients. The training was an absolute triumph.

A few weeks later I was at a meeting with the production manager and during the meeting he told me that he and his colleagues were hugely impressed with what I achieved on the Friday and some of them wanted to stand up and give me a round of applause, but were afraid to do so lest I be embarrassed or upset. This was remarkable by any standard.

The next major challenge with my work was to actually visit the construction sites I'd been working on. One of my clients got the 'fit-out' contracts for some of the Harvey Norman stores around the country and, as their safety consultant, I was given the job of taking care of health and safety on each of the sites. This was going to be a major challenge for me, to go onto male-dominated sites, but I can honestly say that from the start to the finish of each one of these projects I have never had a single problem with the men. On the contrary, some of them paid me the ultimate compliment by referring to me as the *bitch*, whenever they saw me on site or heard that I was due to arrive. Others referred to me as a tough woman. No prizes for guessing how thrilled I was. But the best experience had to be when I was asked out for a drink and invited to dinner, while others asked for my phone number!

It is fair to say that of all the clients I've notified so far, I've not had a problem with a single one of them and in fact, some have told me that I make far more sense as Sara than I ever did in the time they knew me as Tom. This is a wonderful validation and affirmation of who I am and who I will be in the future.

There is, however, no getting away from the fact that my transition did cause a lot of disruption to my business during this period. It was difficult to pay my bills and so on, but I've never run away from that difficulty and have stayed in touch with my creditors. They have been absolutely fantastic towards me and have been very patient. The good news is, that as I complete the various stages of my transition, my business improves and in fact, I'm now able to bring much greater confidence, creativity and motivation to the work I do on behalf of my clients. I am positive that this will only get better.

There could really only one person I would consider travelling with for the first time on my new passport and that was Kathy. We travelled to Spain and stayed for a month. I normally take only one holiday in the year so I try to make the most of it. This holiday was going to be like no other holiday before it. My first hurdle was coping with the check-in at Cork airport, then going through security, then hanging about waiting to board the plane, then being in such close proximity to people for such a long journey and all the while thinking of the many opportunities for being spotted. Then there was the security at Malaga airport and the possibility of being body searched! Can you imagine it? Then there was checking into the hotel, being surrounded by so many guests and the general coming and going for a month, only to go through it all again on my return to Cork; all this for the first time as Sara.

The first good omen I received was in the shape of Kathy's granddaughter Tracy. That child is as cute and can spot things that most adults would be hard pressed to notice. I sat in the back seat of Maureen's car while she drove us to the airport and Tracy and I had the best time playing and all the while she was calling me Sara. When we got to the airport, Tracy wanted to stay with me and we held hands. At one stage Maureen and Kathy took Tracy with them to the toilets, while I was eating my lunch. The next thing I heard was, 'Sara, Sara, where's Sara gone?' You can't imagine how much that gave me a lift and how much confidence it gave me, at least until we reached security. I was certain they would spot me and embarrass me by doing a body search just to be smart. But they didn't stop me and they treated me just like any other passenger going through. They did stop and search Kathy though!

It was plain sailing, or should I say, plain flying from then on. When we got off the plane in Malaga and were walking down the ramp, I heard one of the passengers making reference to recognising me from one of the newspaper articles, that was the only time bar a brief incident in an opticians in Marbella that I had anything like a negative experience; except, that is, for the first day I went out with full make-up on, forgetting that you don't do that in Spain.

On our first full day we travelled up to one of our favourite places, Mijas, to look around and take in some lunch. I swear, I really do think the angels were sent to Spain ahead of me, given the various experiences I had that continually re-affirmed my acceptance as a woman; that day in Mijas was unquestionably one of the best. We went into one the restaurants and all the while I was waiting to be spotted; nothing happened. I was trying to takes pictures of Kathy when the waitress came over and asked if I'd like her to take a picture of us together. I was delighted. Nothing happened. When we were leaving though something did happen, but not at all what I expected. As I was leaving the restaurant to wait outside for Kathy, I was approached by the waiter who had invited us in. 'Hello, you are very nice woman. Where do you stay?' I replied that we were staying in Benalmadena at the Sunset Beach Club.

'May I take you for a drink while you stay?' I told him I'd ask my friend if that was okay as I did not want to be leaving her on her own. 'Thank you and my name is Gerard, what is your name?'

'Sara.'

'It is nice to meet you Sara.' He took my hand and kissed it then kissed me on the cheeks. Wow! And wow again, and again and again. I was on the greatest high. What Gerard did for me that day he will never know; it gave me so much confidence to get through the next day and the day after that.

Every day just got better than the day before and everywhere I went, I was treated as just another woman. That is truly a wonderful thing to experience, to be treated as just another woman, in whatever form that takes. We went to El Corte Inglés in Malaga and spent a great deal of time trying on coats. Kathy found a coat that she particularly liked and spent time trying it on. The store assistant came over to see if we needed any help and stayed with us for quite some time during which I was chatting away to her and trying on some coats myself. Again, it was a totally natural and exhilarating experience. I made some purchases of my own and when I went to pay for my items the lady looked at the name on my credit card and said that my name is *bonito*. This was yet another affirmation of my being a woman.

While we were in Malaga we went to look for a wig shop
we had been to on our last trip. Kathy wanted to try out a different colour for her hair and take a break from using hair
colours. She saw this beautiful honey blonde bob style and
bought it. She looked fabulous in it. When we got back to the
hotel I asked if I could try it on, she said I could and when I
did the reaction was instant. Kathy looked positively shocked
at the transformation and so did I when I looked in the
mirror. It completely transformed my face making it look
more feminine than ever before. It was decided then and
there that I would buy it from her. I wore it for the rest of the
holiday and the effects were only fantastic. So much so that
men everywhere were taking notice, with a few wanting to
know where I was staying so they could meet me for a drink.

One of the funniest incidents was at the Friday market in
the Arroyo de Miel. I was paying for some scarves when the
man giving me my change kept rubbing his hands against
mine and telling me I'm *bonito*. Kathy started to make mis-
chief by telling him that I was single and freely available. He
was delighted to hear it and said, '*in España, you are called
wappa! You are wappa lady!*' I was mortified and went beet-
root red. But I also felt as happy as I could possibly feel,
though at the same time I couldn't help wondering what he
meant when using the word *wappa*? I didn't have to wait to
long to find out. The next time we were in El Corte Inglés I
came across a glossy magazine with the name WAPPA on the
cover, also on the cover was a picture of a beautiful woman,
so there was no need to keep guessing what *wappa* meant
now.

It really didn't matter where we went in Spain over the
month, everywhere we went we were treated as two female

companions on holiday together and it was simply the best possible first holiday for Sara to be on. However it was a hugely emotional time and I can't imagine the amount of emotional and mental energy I used up over that four weeks, except to say that I was absolutely drained and exhausted when I got home. It took me weeks before I was able to get back to work properly.

Doctor Kelly's diagnosis of Gender Identity Disorder has proven to be my salvation, my miracle. Despite the many difficulties, hurts and losses I have had to endure prior to and following my diagnosis, my diagnosis has set me free from a lifetime of internal and external conflict and abject misery and it has opened up a whole new life for me; a life I once only imagined but never believed I would have; the joy of experiencing my own womanhood; something of which I am immensely proud.

I have seen the best and worst of people through this experience. I thought I had experienced prejudice until I made my disclosure and started to live as Sara, but the prejudice I have received since has taught me that even in this third millennium, with all our access to information and education people are as wilfully ignorant, judgmental and intolerant as they have always been and are determined to be. There are, of course, those who have shown nothing but kindness and support, in spite of their not understanding what the condition is. It was enough for them to know who I am and what I'm about. They are the decent people and I am grateful to have met so many of them and to have the love and support of so many with me on this journey towards the woman I always should have been; Sara, Sara-Jane Cromwell. Thank you.